CAREER DIARY

OF A

WEB

DESIGNER

Thirty days behind the scenes
with a professional.

GARDNER'S GUIDE® SERIES

C.R. BELL

GG
C

GARTH GARDNER COMPANY

GGC publishing

Washington DC, USA · London, UK

Cover Designer: Nic Banks
Layout Designer: Rachelle Painchaud-Nash
Editor: Chris Edwards
Publisher: Garth Gardner, Ph.D.

Editorial inquiries concerning this book should be mailed to:
The Editor, Garth Gardner Company, 5107 13th Street N.W.,
Washington DC 20011 or emailed to: info@ggcinc.com.
http://www.gogardner.com

ISBN: 1-58965-022-0

Library of Congress Cataloging-in-Publication Data

Bell, C. R.
    Career diary of a Web designer / C.R. Bell.
    p. cm. -- (Gardner's guide series)
    1. Web sites--Design. 2. Computer graphics. I. Title. II.
Series.

TK5105.888.B447 2006
006.7092--dc22

                                        2005036755

Printed in Canada

TABLE OF CONTENTS

BIOGRAPHY

My name is C. R. Bell and I am a full-time Web Designer for an internationally recognized scientific and educational trade association located in the Washington, D.C metro region. I received my Bachelor of Arts degree in Integrative Studies, with a Minor in Multimedia Design from George Mason University in May 2000.

After I graduated, I took some time to kick back and work in an unstructured environment for a while. During that time, I freelanced as a Web Designer and refined my skills through reading and online tutorials. After enjoying the flexibility of working my own hours for roughly six months, I decided that it was time to get focused and began my search for a full-time job. My goal was to find a job that would allow me to utilize my strengths (creativity, design, writing, and communications). Ideally, I would find a job in the web-design field.

I was initially skeptical that I would be able to find a web-design position, as the country was in the midst of the dot-com collapse and companies were downsizing. As companies started to run out of money, employees were being let go. The result was a job market oversaturated with developers, designers, software programmers, and other professionals with technical backgrounds. My assumption was that most organizations would select an experienced professional over someone fresh out of school if they had to choose.

Despite my concerns, I pushed forward and contacted as many local web-design firms that I was able to locate. In addition, I sent my resume to local consulting agencies and responded to job ads in the newspaper that caught my eye. In the end, I made a strategic decision that paid off – I decided to look in the non-profit sector, on the premise that I could be a big fish in a small pond, rather than a small fish in a big pond. What I mean by that is given the right opportunity, I would likely be one of only a few employees with technical, and more specifically web-design, expertise. As such, I would be expected to contribute to all web projects, and my work would be given a lot of visibility.

The first non-profit organization that showed interest in me and sounded like a good fit, invited me to interview with them on two separate occasions. By the end of the second interview, I felt like my chances of being offered the position were good, and the job sounded promising. Alas, they notified me that they had decided to offer the job to another candidate. As you can imagine, I was quite disappointed with the outcome, but if nothing else, it prepared me for the next step in my search.

In the days and weeks to come, I continued my search through the job postings both in the newspaper and online. After finding several more positions that looked like possibilities, and passing along my resume and relevant information, I finally heard back from someone. That someone was my current employer. They were looking for someone to fill an opening for a full-time web-design position and thought that I might be a good fit.

From that moment on, everything transpired so fast that it was almost a blur. I interviewed with the trade association, and they immediately invited me back for another round. I interviewed with the Executive Director, the Information Technology Director, Director of Programs, and the Publications Manager. The day after my second interview, I was unexpectedly called and offered the position. Everything sounded perfect except for the commute. I would need to drive 25 miles each way, often in unpredictable traffic. My drive could be anywhere from 30 minutes to an hour and a half long. After contemplating my decision overnight, weighing the pros and cons, I decided to accept the offer. That was four and a half years ago.

My preparation for this field was through experience and the courses I took while in college. I decided to begin pursuing the web-design medium during the latter part of my freshman year. While I had taken several computer graphics courses in high school, it wasn't until this point, after attending a short course titled "Introduction to Creating Web Pages," that I realized that this might be my niche.

From that point on, I took any and all web and

multimedia related courses that I was able to sign up for. In my spare time, I created and maintained web pages and tried to learn as much as possible about the medium. Through experimentation and practice, my work started to improve, and the learning curve began to speed up. I also spent a lot of time working through tutorials that I came across on the web and read relevant books and articles. I think that as important as it is to learn the fundamentals of web design, it is equally as important to experiment with new and even sometimes unconventional techniques. By doing so, you get a better feel for what the boundaries of the medium are, what your own boundaries are, and in the process, you become a better designer.

One of my biggest influences was one of my roommates in college who also had an interest in web design and ultimately went on to pursue a career in the same field. There was a healthy competition that existed between us, and it motivated both of us to learn more. Beyond that, I was self-activated.

I believe that I carried a good portion of my formal education with me over to my job, from textbook knowledge to experience. The textbook knowledge gave me a solid foundation, while the hands-on experience has provided me with situation-specific tools and approaches. Ultimately, though, you have to be creative, passionate, and patient to be successful in this field!

CURRENT POSITIONS AND RESPONSIBILITIES

My main function is to maintain the association web site, which consists of over 3,000 individual pages, in addition to updating the staff Intranet, adding content and revising pages as needed. I plan and assist in developing new web-site capabilities, provide approval oversight for our online event submissions database, interact with volunteers, maintain the web site help desk, develop new web tools for staff and the membership, train staff in new web tools when necessary, conduct periodic reviews of all web pages for integrity, work as needed with vendors, and perform routine office procedures as needed.

As the webmaster, I am the primary contact for all web-related inquiries, so I receive a lot of emails and phone calls on related matters. I try to stay current with news and developments in the web-design field and have enhanced my learning by joining the International Webmasters Association (IWA) and the National Association of Photoshop Professionals (NAPP). I also try to stay active in online discussion forums and the blogging community.

When tasked with creating a new web site, I typically handle the project from conception to finish. On any given day, someone may submit a request with a project code provided for me to charge my time to. I will then review the request and figure out roughly how much time will be needed to complete the request. I make sure to let the person making the request know, and then present them with any questions I may have to make sure everyone is on the same page and that no details are overlooked.

All large-scale projects require that a job request form be filled out. On this form, the requestor provides the details of the project, the urgency of the project (in terms of time sensitivity), the requested due date and the date in which the request was submitted.

This information helps me prioritize and makes filing old requests away much easier. Once the completed requests are filed chronologically, they serve as an archive that I can refer to at any time.

I created and maintain the look and feel of the association's homepage and am frequently responsible for creating the functionality and aesthetics of smaller web sites that serve the overall needs of the association and its membership. On some occasions, however, the graphics designers will supply me with a logo or artwork that has been used in one of our publications that they would like to have mirrored on the web. With the needs of the requestor in mind, I apply my judgment and experience to find a solution to the problem or need that has been presented to me. With a solution in mind,

I then work on the aesthetic aspects to make whatever it is I'm working on as visually appealing as possible without sacrificing the functionality.

I will typically create one or more mockup designs in Adobe Photoshop, which I will then export in jpeg or gif format and pass along for review and feedback. Once I receive it, I make any necessary adjustments and then focus on the creation of the web site itself. This process includes the slicing, optimizing, and exporting of images, creating the HTML page itself, creating a template, formatting stylesheets, and adding other scripts (JavaScript, etc.) if the situation calls for it. When a web site requires a database, I will create the database in Microsoft SQL and then incorporate CFML into the code to interact with the database. If the request requires more advanced database work, I will work with one of the web developers to complete the task. The same occurs when the web developers are working on a project that requires a graphical interface, or needs to be cleaned up aesthetically. It's amazing how well we work as a team, and the process is usually fairly fluid. Once all aspects of the request are completed, it is moved to the development server for testing and review.

Once all of the bugs are ironed out and I have obtained final approval from the requestor, the project is migrated over the live server and any links and announcements that are needed get posted.

The software that I use most frequently for my work includes Adobe Photoshop, Adobe Imageready, Adobe Illustrator, Macromedia Fireworks, Macromedia Dreamweaver, Macromedia ColdFusion, and Adobe Acrobat. I am most proficient with Adobe Photoshop, Macromedia Dreamweaver, and Macromedia ColdFusion, though I do try to branch out and get a broader understanding of the techniques used by various designers in the field by experimenting with different programs from time to time. I think it's good to at least explore the possibilities if nothing else.

From time to time, I inherit additional responsibilities, generally on a project by project basis. One of the newest jobs I have been given is creating pdf versions of our conference registration and payment forms, making them editable for the web. I have also advised and contributed to larger projects such as migrating our print publications to electronic format (accessible via the web); served on an exploratory committee looking into the feasibility of conducting our elections in an online format; and assisted in the planning and migration of one of our research publications to CD-ROM format. Other duties range from the creation of web presentations and banner ads, to creating the interfaces for Attendee Message Center and Cyber Café at the association's annual conference.

Typically, there are long-term projects that I'm working

on, but each day can play out much differently than the previous, so day-to-day tasks can vary. I'm not only working for 40 staff members, but also serve the membership at large. I work for 15,000 members that make up 155 different bodies including chapters, sections, and committees, with their own agendas, their own needs, and their own timelines. It's not unusual for a project to be dropped on my lap at a moment's notice. I have certainly learned to become very adaptable and am certainly getting better at prioritizing and planning!

RESUME

EMPLOYMENT

NOVEMBER 1998 – PRESENT

Web Designer, Freelance

Various design projects ranging from banner ads, graphics, to web site design and implementation, to ongoing maintenance and development. Clients include: Home Owner's Association, Non-profit Technical Organization, George Mason University, Graphics Design Company, Professional Development Organization, Online Gift Service.

APRIL 2001 – PRESENT

Web Designer, for an internationally recognized scientific and educational trade association

Redesigned web site twice, enhancing market branding, improving navigation and overall functionality. Responsible for ongoing maintenance and continued development of new capabilities. Provide oversight for online event submissions, develop web tools for staff and membership.

EDUCATION

GEORGE MASON UNIVERSITY

B.A. Integrative Studies, Minor: Multimedia Design, May, 2000

Courses taken includes: Multimedia Development, Website Management, Introduction to Multimedia, HTML Literacy, Multimedia Design, Computing for Artists, Webpage Creation/Design.

EXPERIENCE

Platform / OS:
PC (Windows 95-2000,NT,XP), Macintosh (OS 9)

Languages / Scripts:
HTML, JavaScript, CSS, CFML

Site Design:
Macromedia: ColdFusion 5, Dreamweaver 4/MX, Microsoft: FrontPage 98-2000

Graphics/Multimedia:
Adobe: Acrobat, Illustrator, Imageready, Photoshop
Macromedia: Fireworks, Flash

Browsers:
Internet Explorer 5.x/6, Netscape 4.x/6-8, Mozilla, Firefox, Opera

Other:
Telnet, FTP

AWARDS

Winter, 2004 – Award for "Outstanding Initiative, Creativity and Customer Service"

Fall, 2002 – "Industry Standard of Excellence" Web Recognition Award, for association website.

Spring, 2002 – Award for "Outstanding Performance and Dedication", for redesign of association website.

Fall, 2001 – Winner of logo contest for local recreational organization.

Spring, 1999 – Web page entered into Innovations 99 Exhibition

MEMBERSHIP

2001 – Present – National Association of Photoshop Professionals (NAPP)

2001 – Present – International Webmasters Association (IWA)

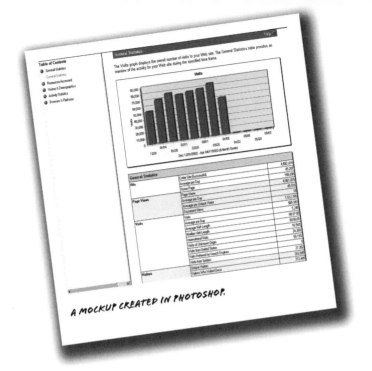

A MOCKUP CREATED IN PHOTOSHOP.

Day 1 | JANUARY 27

PREDICTIONS

- Work on mailing list configurations.
- Review Majordomo documentation.
- Review web site to verify recent conversion to server side includes.

DIARY

I started the day at 7:00 a.m. as I would any other, checking the webmaster inbox for new emails and responding to

---

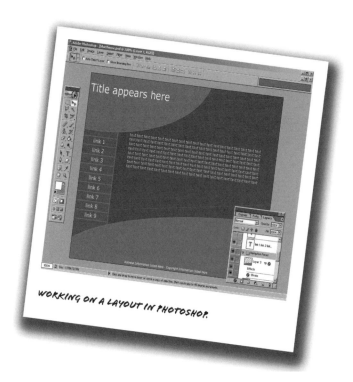

WORKING ON A LAYOUT IN PHOTOSHOP.

member inquiries. After that, I checked for newly submitted entries to our online events database and reviewed them for authenticity and errors prior to approval. Once I approve submissions, they are automatically viewable and searchable via the web site. They are also added to the queue to be printed in the next month's issue of our membership magazine.

After completing some of the more routine tasks I decided to look over some of the documentation on Majordomo, the *mailing list management software we are using. It was set up by one of our volunteers and is in the process of being handed over to me to manage remotely.*

Several job requests were waiting for me, so I decided to tackle them and take a break from reviewing the Majordomo documentation. The first request, from the Careers Coordinator, had some revisions for the online career center. She also emailed me a new version of a careers presentation that she created in PowerPoint to be placed online.

A lot of the work I do on a daily basis revolves around adding to and revising content already on the web. Unlike in a web-design firm, I am working solely for my employer, and my services are not being contracted out to other clients. On the flip-side, much like in a web-design firm, I do get to work on a variety of web sites (in size and nature), create mockups and graphics, and coordinate with other web developers and outside vendors on a regular basis. I also work for 40 staff members and 15,000 members.

After returning from lunch around noon, I got word from the Meetings and Events Department that we would be scrapping our online registration process due to technical problems on the part of the vendor. This was a major setback in terms of convenience and money spent, but the best decision in the long run. Members were frustrated to the point where they were no longer registering because the process was so problematic. Luckily, I had already been tasked with creating

CREATING AN EDITABLE FORM IN ADOBE ACROBAT.

an editable form in pdf format that could be mailed in once filled out. Unfortunately, this decision required me to make revisions to the Meeting and Events site, the association homepage, and the pdf registration form itself to reflect the change. I guess I'll be busy tomorrow!

By the time I was briefed on what the plan was, 3:00 had already passed. Before I left for the day, I submitted my equipment request for a new mouse (Microsoft Optical) and a keyboard (Microsoft Natural Keyboard). Once I got my boss's signature, I submitted the request and headed home.

LESSONS/PROBLEMS

I essentially accomplished what I set out to do today. Through my experience, I have learned that prioritizing is a must and attention must be given to the most important or time-sensitive project, as something unexpected always arises. I also know that my day does not necessarily end when I leave the physical workplace. There aren't enough hours in a day or days in a week to get done what needs to get done. My mind is always going, creating, and visualizing. Web design is a great outlet to burn this creative energy and all the while, put it to work for me.

LEAVING THE BUILDING, HEADING FOR THE PARKING LOT.

Day 2 | *JANUARY 28*

PREDICTIONS

- *Address search-engine functionality.*
- *Work on registration form (pdf) for conference and revise web site where necessary.*

DIARY

Today I decided to spend a little time looking into improving the search function on our web site. Up until now we've used

Microsoft Internet Information Server (IIS)'s built-in search engine. While it was customizable and worked, it is not providing the quality search results that users have grown accustomed to as a result of the efforts of Google, Yahoo!, Atomz, Teoma, etc.

I decided to give Google's free site search feature a try, which allows for limited customization, to see if it would yield better search results than our current engine. The setup was fairly simple (web interface) and modifying the code to build it into the existing site was easy, too. After completing the initial setup, I tested it out and I immediately noticed a significant improvement. The search results were more accurate and better descriptions were being pulled from the HTML pages and pdf documents.

Before I ask to purchase a fully customizable version of the search feature, I want to test the current setup out for a couple months to see what kind of feedback I receive and gauge whether or not the inquiries decrease, and whether documents are being located more easily. If all goes well, I will look into purchasing the fully customizable site search to make it appear more seamless to users and more consistent with the rest of the web site's look and feel.

The end of the day rapidly approached and I could already see that my afternoon was going to be consumed with revisions to the meeting's registration form (pdf) and revising the web site itself. As expected, the registration system that was in place was taken down, and the web developers in-house worked to

MY NEW BOOK ARRIVED TODAY!

complete a less sophisticated and scaled down system to
replace it for the time being. It was to be done by 3:00 p.m.
This was no small task, considering it was assigned yesterday
and it's already 12:00 p.m. and the project hasn't been
started yet. However, if anyone can pull it off, our lead
developer can. Luckily for me, all I was asked to do was replace
verbiage, update the instructions for users, and modify the pdf
version of the registration form. It would have been a lot easier
of course if I had not left the source file at home on my
personal computer! I ended up having to recreate the

document (importing graphics, redoing the editable fields) as it needed to be done today by 3:00 p.m. as well.

At about 2:45 p.m., our Assistant Director called to say that the web developers had finished the replacement online registration form and asked how much longer I would need to complete my work. I told him I would probably need about 30 more minutes. Needless to say, this was 15 minutes too long. Apparently, we had indicated to members that all of the new forms would be available for use by 3:00 p.m. and we needed to stick to this deadline.

It was time to kick it into high gear. My initial plan to create an aesthetically pleasing and ultra user-friendly outline of the "steps to complete registration" had to be put on the back burner, and instead replaced with a skeleton of my original design – providing simply the wording. I finished by 3:05 p.m., and we rolled out the newly revised registration forms. I hung around to clean up some code and place an announcement on the homepage informing users that the changes had been completed and headed for home around 3:30. What had started out as a well-paced day turned into a frantic craze to make ends meet before a spontaneous deadline expired!

I stopped by the mailroom on the way out and to my surprise; a package was waiting for me. It was a book I ordered (Adobe Photoshop 7 Web Design with GoLive 6 by Michael Baumgardt). It got great reviews and looked like it had a lot of useful information in it, which influenced my decision to purchase it. With book in hand, I was out the door!

LESSONS/PROBLEMS

Today I definitely learned that I could meet a deadline (okay, so I missed it by 5 minutes—give me a break!). I also realized that sometimes you have to settle with the bare minimum and readdress items at a later time if the situation necessitates it (it hurts to be a perfectionist!). I think I accomplished what I set out to, but I sort of anticipated what was coming (but not when!). Unfortunately, I did have a mini-crisis after leaving the source file that needed updating at home, but was able to work something out in the end. It happens to the best of us. I expect tomorrow to go a bit smoother.

PREDICTIONS

- Test the new registration system and finish revisions.
- Test beta CD of presented paper compilation.
- Look into training, potential courses to further knowledge.

DIARY

After scalding my throat with my morning coffee, I tested the new registration system to see if I could "blow it up" and to make sure the instructions read clearly. I gave it a run through and had no problems whatsoever. One thing that you need to do when testing is revert to your "newbie" self.

You need to account for everyone from the person who has never used a computer to the more advanced user who skips the instructions all together. Any ridiculous question you can come up with will be asked. People simply don't think alike and interact with the web differently. That said, trying to get in the mind of a user who is not very familiar with the web is an art in itself and requires you to detach yourself from all that you have learned and know about the web, thus the reverting to your "newbie" self.

Not too long after I did this, Susan came in with more revisions to be made on the Meetings and Events web page. It sometimes amazes me how people treat the web so much differently than they would print. While the web provides *advantages of quick distribution and easy publishing, it seems to have given people the sense that something is better than nothing (whether full of mistakes or error-free) and that you can simply make infinite revisions until you get it right. Whereas with a print publication, a document must be in the final form by the time it goes to print. I have taken steps to try and get coworkers to have their material in final form prior to submitting it to me, but sometimes there is little I can do. It's tough to justify, when there is no cost incurred to revise the content and when it's technically never unchangeable.*

At around 11:30, I completed my revisions, checked my email, and moved on to the next project. The association recently created a minority directory that individuals can search on to find members of the industry who are minorities. To be included in the directory, association members must voluntarily submit an online survey first. The committee charged with creating this project worked with one of our web developers to code the project and it recently went live and was advertised in our membership publication. Someone raised some ethical issues, so the committee asked that some revisions be made, changing some of the requirements to perform a search, adding a disclaimer that users must agree to, and changing some navigational components. I was tasked with making these changes. This gave me an opportunity to work with ColdFusion, which up until this point, I had limited knowledge of.

Today was the first day for our new graphic designer. The person in this position tends to be the liaison or bridge between myself and the Communications department. This means that I will likely be getting to know the new staff member pretty well as time goes by. I look forward to getting a new perspective and hearing some new ideas. Before leaving for the day, I spent the last 30 minutes looking through various training catalogs for courses that might interest me.

LESSONS/PROBLEMS

Overall I had a productive day, but the duplication of efforts caused me to grow a little frustrated. On the flip side, it was nice that I got the opportunity to work on a project that was not my creation. It's always a challenge to work on other people's code as everyone has their own techniques and habits when it comes to the way they lay out the code and the approaches they take.

MY DESK.

Day 4 | *JANUARY 31*

PREDICTIONS

- I'll go into the office for at least a half day to take care of a few outstanding job requests.
- Clean up some directories on my computer and on the network.

DIARY

Since I was out ill yesterday, I decided to come in to the office and work for at least the morning. Fridays are normally my telecommuting day, but I wanted to take care of any job requests that might be sitting in my inbox and finish up the minority directory project. The association recently began giving employees the option to work an alternative work schedule, and if appropriate, the option to telecommute one or two days a week. So beginning in July, I elected to telecommute once a week and it has been great. I can do everything from home that I can do at work and don't have to worry about the commute. The only downside is that there is less face-to-face interaction, but it is usually pretty quiet in the office on Fridays anyhow. The other two web developers (Mike and Kelly) telecommute one day a week, leaving only two days during the week that we are all in-house. Amazingly, there have been very few snags or crises that have arisen as a result of our schedules. It does require that we communicate effectively, but so far it has been quite manageable.

I got into the office around 6:45 and had several job requests waiting for me, so I logged in to the network and got right to work. One of the requests I received was to create a web photo album for pictures from the venue where our annual conference will be taking place this summer. To give staff a better idea of the space they'll have to work with, the Meetings and Events staff took digital photos to show them since it was not feasible (or cost effective) for everyone to do a site visit. Sometimes I find that the simple projects are the most fun. Perhaps it's simply having some variety every now and then, or maybe it's just being able to complete a task

TELECOMMUTING PROPOSAL
C.R. BELL – Web Designer
April 4, 2002

Business Needs of IRSETA:
In regards to my position, the ability to act as the primary interface for members, staff, and the public in dealings revolving the web site, the ability to create, modify and make additions to the web site, maintain the online help desk (troubleshooting and problem-solving web-related issues, and maintaining Webmaster email). Provide approval oversight for online event submissions. Interact with the volunteers.

Appropriateness of job responsibilities for telecommuting:
The job responsibilities of the Web Designer are appropriate for telecommuting, and can be performed in full from a remote location. Since I would be reachable via email and telephone as usual, there will be no drop-off in communication. All web maintenance can be performed remotely as well.

The employee's needs:
To relieve some of the commuting issues as a result of traveling to and from Fairfax on a daily basis. All of my tasks can be performed from home, and I don't feel I am needed to be in-house full-time.

Compatibility of employee to telecommuting:
I am setup to work from home already. I have a computer, DSL Internet connection, and necessary software.

The equipment requirements, workspace design considerations, and scheduling hours:
I have all the equipment needed to fulfill my responsibilities. The only items I might need are general office supplies (pencils, paper, paper clips, CDs for backing up, etc.). No special design considerations need to be taken. I have a suitable workspace, and there should be no scheduling conflicts.

Tax implications:
Not aware of any.

THE PROPOSAL THAT I WROTE AND SUBMITTED TO MANAGEMENT TO REQUEST THE OPTION OF TELECOMMUTING EACH WEEK.

quickly. The other job requests pertained to the annual conference site, adding additional information and placing some pdfs online for members.

At around noon, I decided that I had done enough to catch up and headed home to telecommute for the rest of the day. When I arrived at my apartment, I had several emails waiting for me. I made a few more minor revisions to the minority directory and then transferred it over from the development server to the live server. Finally, I sent an email to the committee involved, to confirm the completion of those revisions.

Before long, the day was coming to a close. One of the last emails I read was a request to design a web site for one of our smaller meetings. The plan is to meet next week to brainstorm.

LESSONS/PROBLEMS

I was glad I went in for a portion of the day as I was able to knock a lot out, but was also glad I was able to work from home in the afternoon, avoiding the Friday rush hour. It's certainly nice to have the flexibility that telecommuting has given me. I'm excited about getting the opportunity to create another web site and that will be my primary goal for next week.

PREDICTIONS

- Post teasers for membership publication.
- Handle any job requests in my inbox.
- Respond to email and phone inquiries.

DIARY

Today started out pretty quiet, which is always a great way to start a Monday. I was able to tackle some of my more routine tasks early on in the day. I revised an event submission in our online events database for a member and reviewed the new submissions. I had a few job requests to take care of so I decided to get a jump on them. The first couple entailed adding information to already existing pages and another required me to change information (yet again!) on the meeting's web site and mail-in registration form. After completing those, I decided to look into a small issue related to the minority search form. I had to consult with Kelly to figure out a solution, but all in all it was a pretty easy fix. With that resolved, hopefully that project is finished.

Before I headed out to lunch around 11:30, I received an email from the editor of one of our our educational newsletters. He recently spoke with me via telephone about creating a new web site that would contain a complete archive of past newsletters since its inception. During our phone call, several questions were raised as to what I could do in regards to long-term maintenance and how much content could be stored in-house (server space restrictions). In both cases, I was able to give him optimistic responses. I told him to gather all the data for the site and to send it to me, at which time we could discuss how we would go about displaying the data and creating the necessary navigation for it. After that, I will create one or more mockups that will be tweaked until a final design is agreed upon. At that time, we will roll out the site for public use. His email today was to confirm the mailing of a zip disk with the old issues and an update on his progress in organizing the data to make it navigable. I should be hearing from him again later in the week.

At lunch I learned that Lisa, the Careers Coordinator and friend (not to mention one of only a few close to me in terms of age) of mine, was resigning from her position at the association and would be taking a new position elsewhere. Her last day is in two weeks. I had mixed feelings in that I will miss her companionship, but am happy she found something that would allow her to grow professionally. She also happened to be one of the most organized and detail-oriented members of the staff who cared a great deal about our web presence and assisted me in many ways. Her absence will definitely be felt.

After returning from a long lunch with her around 1:00, I ran into Mike, our lead web developer on the way inside and he brought up an email I had sent a few weeks back (can you tell he's a busy man?) regarding cross-platform and cross-browser issues and our web site. The email revolved around some outstanding issues that we needed to discuss; the game plan is to meet on Wednesday to discuss the problems and hopefully come up with some feasible solutions. To briefly explain the issue(s), there are a great number of browsers that are or are not compliant with today's web standards and interpret code differently. A lot of our members work at educational institutions, thus use Unix systems to access the web site. At last year's annual conference, I overheard that some Unix-based browsers crash upon reaching our web site. I can pretty much ascertain that it relates to the one of the JavaScript components that we have incorporated into the site. Those two components are the browser sniffer (which detects the browser and platform and calls the respective stylesheet) and the JavaScript fly-out menu. We need to figure out how severe the problem is, if we can set up some sort of testing environment to troubleshoot such issues, determine whether or not we can fix it without removing the JavaScript, or if it should be taken out in its entirety. Basically, we need to identify, evaluate, and then react accordingly. It doesn't appear to be a widespread problem, but being the perfectionist that I am, I would like to remedy the problem if at all possible. I'm optimistic that we will be able to figure something out. Before I left, he also mentioned that a vendor would be here on Wednesday and that he may want my presence as it pertains to our online e-commerce modules and a potential replacement for it.

I spent the rest of the afternoon cleaning up various pages and perusing the site for outdated and irrelevant content. One final request rolled in from the Communications Department. It was the teasers and accompanying artwork from our membership magazine that I post monthly to entice people to join the association. At one point we discussed putting full issues online but decided it best to simply place featured items and brief teasers so members and non-members could preview what is in the latest and archived issues. Once I completed creating and uploading the teasers, I packed my bag up and headed for the door.

LESSONS/PROBLEMS

Lesson 1: Nothing is certain: whether it be technology as a whole, more specifically the web medium, or life in general.

Lesson 2: Rely on others. Nobody has all of the answers. If possible, consult with peers or someone with more knowledge and experience than yourself to bounce ideas off of.

I had a very productive day and made progress on several fronts. I was sad to hear that Lisa will be leaving, but was glad to hear she was "moving on up." I think this week will start to pick up but will remain productive.

PREDICTIONS

- Run WebTrends report for advertising on one of our publication's homepage.
- Continue to scour site for pages needing updates.
- Look through newly acquired book.

DIARY

Today started out much like yesterday, nice and quiet. I decided my first task of the day would be to go through the web site and look for broken links and outdated content. I updated pages as needed and emailed staff to get input on issues that needed their help. I reorganized the staff roster, revised the FAQ, added entries to the "404 Best Bets" function (a script that displays titles of web pages that users might be trying to reach – instead of the standard "Page Not Found" when an invalid link is entered).

After that, I updated an announcement for the Education Manager and then optimized some graphics that the graphic designer emailed over to go along with the membership magazine teasers I posted yesterday.

I really love the "Save for Web" feature in Photoshop. I think it's been around since version 6, but it has made my life a lot simpler when it comes to crunching down file size without compromising image quality. Prior to this, one had to manually do the work, which wasn't impossible, but took longer and to me, felt less efficient.

After taking lunch at 12:00, I returned feeling inspired, so I decided to do some benchmarking on what other associations were doing with their web sites mainly in terms of aesthetics and organization of content. Not that I think I'm going to redesign the web site anytime soon (but I hope to down the line!), but if I find something that someone else is doing that is very effective or that users seem to be responding well to, why not do it for our members? I believe that as a designer you need to stay informed and look at what others are doing and pay attention to trends.

By the time I was done, I probably perused about 30 or so web sites. Some were cutting edge, some simply efficient, and some were disasters. Overall I felt that our site was at least better than average if not great. There are certainly a lot worse! I think there is always room for improvement, but hey – we did receive a "Standard of Excellence" Web Recognition Award in 2002, so we must be doing something right!

I took notes on some things I came across that were of interest to me. I wouldn't mind exploring some of them further at least to be informed. One thing I noticed in the past but was reminded of today was the lack of a "Job Openings" or "Careers at XYZ" page where people visiting the web site can find information on job openings at our organization. I sent an email to Human Resources to ask if this had ever been considered and to let her know (for whatever it was worth), that I felt it would be a useful addition. So we will see what happens. Three o'clock crept up on me today but came as a nice surprise. I got a lot done but was ready to go home.

LESSONS/PROBLEMS

I didn't get to run the WebTrends report for the editor as I got sidetracked with other things. After doing some benchmarking I have a lot of ideas and want to do some more exploring. Tomorrow I meet with Mike to discuss outstanding web issues and listen to a vendor presentation on alternatives to our online e-commerce system.

PREDICTIONS

- Meet with Mike to discuss problems and possible resolutions.
- Run site WebTrends.
- Vendor presentation.
- More benchmarking and brainstorming.

DIARY

Today when I got in, the zip disk that the editor of the educational newsletter mailed me was waiting for me in my mailbox. When I went up to my office and opened up the disk, I was pleased to see that all of the archived newsletters were in pdf form and titled in such a way that I wouldn't need to open them to figure out which volume and issue they were. I sent an email to the editor to inform him that I received the zip disk and would be awaiting his verbiage and additional information for the web site I will be creating for the newsletter.

Not long after, I received an instant message from Kelly, our other web developer, who was telecommuting today. She said that our development server was hung up and asked if I could go downstairs to the computer room and reboot the machine. I told her I would take care of it and made my way down to the computer room. Once I restarted the server and returned to my desk, I informed Kelly that the server was back online. Although not officially sanctioned, a lot of the staff use MSN Messenger to communicate with each other. It's quite effective *for quick questions, group conversations, and is a lot simpler than pulling up a new email window to type a message or picking up a phone and playing phone tag with people when they aren't at their desks. Its role has become increasingly more important in light of the association's adaptation of telecommuting and alternate work schedules. It permits several of us to stay in contact even when not in the office and has come in handy on several occasions.*

Someone recently brought an article to my attention that discussed spam and a technique that although not full-proof, had been somewhat effective in preventing "spiders" from harvesting email addresses from web sites. Since all staff get junk email on a regular basis, and since we publish our contact information on the web site for the world to see, I decided to read the article and give one of the techniques a shot. Basically all that it entailed was replacing the "@" symbol in the HTML code with "@." This would confuse the spider in to thinking it was not a valid email address, but would appear as it should to anyone who perused the site. Unfortunately, I have no real means by which to find out if it has prevented additional junk email from being sent to staff, but I can at least rest knowing that I have responded to new information that I have obtained. I am also skeptical as I know that anytime someone creates or finds a counter-measure for attacks (whether it's viruses, hacks, backdoors, spam, etc.), someone else finds another hole to exploit or backdoor to break through.

After squeezing in a quick lunch around 12:30, a

representative from Active Matter arrived and we met to discuss our current e-commerce system, the problems we have been having with it, and to explore what options they have available to us if we were to go with them in the future. The meeting was initially only supposed to take 30 minutes, but ended up lasting one and a half hours. We had recently been burned by our last vendor, so Dave and Mike were both asking very detailed and important questions that in some cases was difficult for the vendor to answer. We were given demos of several of their products and were able to have a lot of our questions answered. We found out that several other clients of our previous vendor had migrated over to Active Matter due to their dissatisfaction with our current vendor's service. At the end of the meeting, the vendor said they would work on writing up a contract and will send it over to us next week to look over and decide ifwe are interested in moving forward with them. Overall I came out of the meeting with a good feeling about the vendor. I found out that if we were to go with them, their product would allow for much more customization than our previous vendors did because their code is not encrypted. To me, this would definitely be a plus, as one never knows when customization might be needed down the line. The more flexibility given to us, the better.

After the meeting was over, I went back to my office and did a little testing with some JavaScript that I came upon while surfing the web, in addition to making some minor updates to the association's by-laws and adding some information to an awards page for the current year.

LESSONS/PROBLEMS

I felt pretty optimistic about getting our e-commerce system up with the new vendor. They sounded like they were pretty confident, and from what I could tell, it didn't seem like false bravado. They had actual working demos for us to test and look at and were even willing to give us a client list so we could contact them and get their opinions on Active Matter's services. They had answers to almost all of the questions asked of them, and the few that they were unable to answer they promised to research and get back to us on once they sent us the completed contract.

PREDICTIONS

- All-staff meeting.
- See what I can squeeze in with time left over.

DIARY

The entire first half of the day was exhausted by our monthly all-staff meeting, where we share important developments that have come up throughout the organization in the previous month. We typically start out by sharing staff announcements, birthdays and anniversaries, introduce any new staff members, and then give the floor to managers of the various departments so they can share important developments and give updates relevant to all staff. I generally don't have much to contribute, as most web-related issues are announced via email or they are discovered when browsing the web. Each month someone is assigned to take notes, but I was off the hook this go around. The highlight of this month's meeting was getting to see the floor plan and interior decorating selections for our new building (due to be completed in the fall). Right now we reside in a beat up, 5-floor, 40 year-old building. Did I mention that my office is about the size of a utility closet (at least everyone else in the office thinks so) with no windows? The space doesn't bother me so much, as I have plenty of room to maneuver and can get my job done. I do wish I could see what's going on outside from time to time, but

I look at it as one less distraction and a reason to get up and walk around every so often. By the time the staff meeting concluded it was already lunchtime, so I decided to get some food and then try to salvage part of the day to get some work done.

When I returned around 12:00, I burned a CD for a coworker, set up a meeting with the Barbara to discuss reorganizing the content on the education portion of the web site, and responded to some email inquiries that had come in. Susan came in to discuss details regarding a web site she wanted me to create for a small conference she was in charge of. She brought me all of the verbiage and content to build the site around and said that I could go any direction that I wanted to in terms of aesthetics, and also that she was leaving it in my hands. She said that the Communications department was working on the logos and getting the registration forms together and would be sending them over to me once they are completed. I told her that sounded fine and that I would start working on it right away. Before she left she mentioned that there was another conference in the works and that Stu, our Executive Director, asked that a web site be created for that in addition. I told her that this was not a problem and in fact that I welcomed the additional work, as it's what I love to do. This of course made her day and with that I went home.

LESSONS/PROBLEMS

Considering the amount of time I had to actually get some work done, I think I faired pretty well, but as you can see, much of my day was consumed by the mandatory staff meeting. Luckily, we only have them once a month. They typically only take about an hour, but this one took longer due to the briefing on our new building and the question and answer session that came as a result. Every once in a while it's nice to have a day that demands a little less than the daily grind, but the downside is not having time to put a dent in anything very significant. Tomorrow I get to telecommute, which will give me some peace and quiet and the opportunity to be more productive and hopefully recoup some of the time lost today.

PREDICTIONS

- Get started on the annual conference web site – brainstorm, come up with a mockup.
- Respond to email inquiries.

DIARY

Today I woke up in a winter wonderland. I looked outside and discovered that 4-6 inches of snow had fallen overnight, which caused the government to issue a 2-hour delayed opening. Since my employer follows the government's leave policy, this also affected us. This didn't affect me very much since I was already working from home, but it at least meant the first couple hours of the day would be a bit more relaxed. Most staff that I normally communicate with via instant messenger and email will not arrive until at least 9:00 am, so I decided to make some coffee, turn on the news, and knock out some of the more administrative tasks.

When 9:00 finally rolled around, people started to pop up on instant messenger, and emails slowly started to fill my inbox. I decided to shift gears and begin to work on my main objective for the day, which was to come up with some sort of design for the annual conference web site. Sounds simple doesn't it? I spent the better portion of the day experimenting and creating several mockups, before deciding on one I liked more than the others. Once I settled on the one I liked the most, I moved

THE SNOW DRIFT THAT ACCUMULATED OUTSIDE MY APARTMENT'S SLIDING DOOR. GOOD THING TODAY WAS A TELECOMMUTING DAY!

from Adobe Photoshop to Adobe Imageready, where I carefully sliced up the design and exported the images. At that point, I opened up Macromedia ColdFusion and worked on the HTML to pull the components together. I have been using ColdFusion more recently in an effort to become more proficient with it. Unlike Dreamweaver, ColdFusion does not give you the ability to lay out your webpage visually in addition to providing a window for editing the code directly. ColdFusion requires you to rely on your hand-coding skills, but is a powerful application if you really familiarize yourself with its features. I have found *that by using both, I get the best of both worlds. Oftentimes I will lay out the initial design in Dreamweaver, and then jump over to ColdFusion to clean up the code. ColdFusion has given me greater flexibility in terms of separating pages into pieces. I am able to create and maintain a single header and footer file, which wraps around the individual pages where content varies. It makes for easier maintenance and updating, and also makes the code a lot cleaner.*

WORKING ON SOME CODE IN COLDFUSION.

AN EXAMPLE OF A BRIEF MOCKUP LAID OUT IN PHOTOSHOP.

When quitting time rolled around, I had managed to complete a basic skeleton web site for the annual meeting. I was even able to populate the web site with content provided to me by Susan and migrate it over to the development server testing and review. I decided to hold off on sending an email to Susan, to give myself a little more time to polish up the aesthetics and refine the code a little more. First thing on Monday, I will work on cleaning the site up and hopefully pass it along for review.

LESSONS/PROBLEMS

The two-hour delayed opening caused the day to start out a little slowly, but it allowed me to take care of some of the more administrative tasks. The good news, however, was that I managed to hammer out a skeleton web site, beginning from the conception, all the way to the actual production stage. To top it off I was able to populate the site with actual content provided to me by Susan, so I was off to a great start! By the time the day ended, I was feeling pretty burned out, so I thought it a good idea to hold off on notifying Susan that the site was ready for review. I'd rather wait and decide that nothing else needs to be done, than to pass it along prematurely.

PREDICTIONS

- *Work on a web site for smaller conference.*
- *Follow up on progress of educational newsletter.*

DIARY

Today looked like it might be a repeat of Friday based on the weather forecasts, but luckily (or unluckily depending on how you look at it) the snow wasn't sticking to the roads, making the commute to work a little less treacherous. You have to love the uncertain winter weather patterns of the Northeast!

When I finally made it to work, there was a package waiting for me. Sure enough, it was the design books that I recently ordered. Included with the books was a solicitation inviting me to join a new "design book club." It seemed enticing as it was set up to function much like Columbia House, where you receive a catalog once a month, with one selection highlighted, requiring you to mail in the card if you are not interested in that month's selection. The great part was that it looked like they had a lot of big name books and they only asked for $16.00 to receive 5 books! There aren't many places that you will find allow you to buy new books for those prices. I will need to set aside some time to peruse their offerings to see if I can find any diamonds in the rough.

SOME OF THE MANY BOOKS I HAVE ACQUIRED AND FREQUENTLY REFER TO ON A DAILY BASIS. I HAVE FOUND BOOKS TO BE ONE OF MY FAVORITE TOOLS WHEN LEARNING NEW SKILLS OR TECHNIQUES.

After I finished looking over my new books, I opened up Microsoft Excel and filled out my timesheet for the previous week. We have to be very specific when logging our time, indicating which project code to bill our time to. This can be somewhat tedious, but is important in determining labor distribution. The majority of my time is charged to a generic project code titled "Web," which covers most of the routine maintenance and day-to-day tasks that I perform. For projects brought to me by specific departments (i.e., Education, Meetings, and Events), I am provided a project code that is more specific to the project being given to me. The plus side of the project code system is that it allows my supervisor and I to keep track of what it is specifically that I spend my time working on.

Once I turned in my timesheet, I loaded up Photoshop and began working on a new mockup for a smaller conference that the association will be holding soon. For this design, I decided to be a little more flexible in terms of the aesthetics. I felt like I had a little more room to experiment since it was for a smaller conference, which meant it would be less visible than some of my other projects. For example, I selected colors that I might not normally use and incorporated a more simplified navigation. It definitely helped that there wasn't quite as much content that needed to populate the site as there was with the annual conference web site.

For the most part, the design was in good shape, but I now needed to export it from Photoshop and begin working on the code in ColdFusion.

By around 11:30 (lunchtime!), I was in pretty good shape. I finished slicing the design up, exported the graphics, and got the code in order. All that was left to do when I returned from lunch was to create the background image, work on the cascading stylesheet that would accompany the web site, and finally email Susan to get her feedback.

Once I completed the missing pieces, I checked on my email and discovered that the editor of educational newsletter had sent me an outline for how he wanted the web site archive to be laid out. The outline basically consisted of a list of the major navigational elements of the site, followed by their corresponding sub-headings and relevant links below that.

I decided to create a mockup based on the editor's outline, first selecting a color scheme that I wanted to weave throughout the site, building off of that.

It still surprises me how much flexibility I'm given as a designer. I have found that most people are pleased when you tell them that what they envision is feasible and are ultimately willing to give the reigns to me when it comes to deciding what direction to go creatively. It allows me to do what I feel I do best and motivates me to try and deliver a product that exceeds their needs if possible.

It's a compliment, a challenge, and a confidence booster when someone defers to my judgment. While I am the Web Designer, it doesn't always guarantee that I will be given the freedom to do what I feel is best. I've learned through my freelance work that there are some people who believe that their vision is the best (and often only) way and are unwilling to deviate from that vision. As a result, I've grown to be grateful for the opportunities given to me, where I am able to apply my knowledge and experience to find a solution or build what is being requested of me.

Based on the outline sent to me by the newsletter editor, I created a basic mockup of how I thought the site should look, *then pulled it into Imageready and sliced it up. I went through the steps I usually go through, optimizing the images for the web, saving them, switching over to ColdFusion to work on the code, and building the template for the site to be built from. At that point, I populated the web site with some filler content to give the editor a better idea of what the page will look like once live, and then placed it on the development server for review. When I finished, I emailed the editor to get his feedback and also to find out what his plans were for the content that resided on the old newsletter homepage. After that, I packed up and headed out to brave the cold.*

LESSONS/PROBLEMS

Today was a great day! I felt extremely productive and came up with one very solid design and got a good start on a second one. I'm always excited when I complete a project and get to see it in its final form. There is also a feeling of suspense as I wait to see and hear how others react to it. I hope for the best, but keep an open mind. You have to be or you'll never survive in this field. You can't take criticism personally; you have to go in knowing that everyone sees things differently, and there is never only one solution to a problem or request.

The day went by quickly, perhaps too quickly. I am looking forward to coming in tomorrow and picking up where I left off with the newsletter web site. Hopefully I will have heard from the editor by that time with his feedback, and with any luck, he'll be pleased with what I come up with so far!

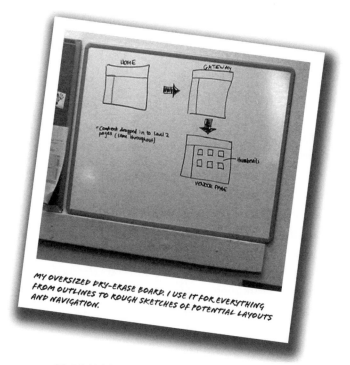

MY OVERSIZED DRY-ERASE BOARD. I USE IT FOR EVERYTHING FROM OUTLINES TO ROUGH SKETCHES OF POTENTIAL LAYOUTS AND NAVIGATION.

Day 11 | **FEBRUARY 11**

PREDICTIONS

- Work on the newsletter web site.
- Meet with Barbara to discuss redesign of Education page.

DIARY

Today I came in and immediately began working on the newsletter web site. I received a response from the editor with answers to my questions. With answers in hand, I was able to move forward, focusing on getting the final design together.

I spent the first few hours trying to complete a few minor aesthetic details to round out the design. A lot of times I like to add a few minor accents to a design, once the overall framework is in place, with the stylesheet completed. A photo here or there, graphical headers, and other visual cues can enhance a sites overall aesthetics greatly. I suggest just playing around with different ideas, plugging things in and swapping them out until you find something that you think works. It's basically a lot of trial and error. After not having a lot of success there, I decided that I needed to move the menu bar down so it would balance the rest of the page. I improved the navigation further by making each button on the menu a rollover. This will also provide a visual cue to the user as to which button their cursor is on.

By the time I finished altering the navigational elements, 10:00 rolled around and I had an appointment with Barbara to discuss redesigning the Education homepage on the association web site. The meeting lasted about 30 minutes and was quite productive. I came out of the meeting with some preliminary outlines, sketched out as to how we wanted to reorganize the content to make it more user-friendly. Our goal is to improve the page's organization, reduce the overall clutter, and make it easier to navigate. Currently, users have to wade through a lot of junk to get to what they really want. The goal for the redesign is to hook users in early on in by presenting them with key elements of education (i.e., K-3, 4-6, 7-12, Middle School Teachers, etc.), so that they will find the key area that applies to them and then will be taken to the content they most likely will want to see. Barbara plans to take a look at what's already on the Education homepage and plans to map out how she would like it organized and then I will have a go at it. Once I complete the revisions, I will put the new page on the development server for feedback and tweak it from there. All in all it should make the page much more organized and easier to use.

After lunch, I got word from Susan that she had looked at the initial web site that I created for her meeting and was quite pleased. She thought it was great and had no immediate revisions that she wanted to make. She did have some additional content she wanted to incorporate, but other than that it was ready to be passed on to the conference's organizing committee for their feedback. She also mentioned to me that Stu asked that she talk to me about having another web site created for a meeting that he was specifically involved with. Apparently it is needed ASAP as the meeting takes place in May, and registration opens in March! Luckily, I work well under pressure, but I learned that she apparently took it upon herself to tell Stu that I had already started on the project (when in fact I only found out about the project today!). Oh well, guess I better get moving!

The last thing I planned to do today was transfer over a web site, housing biographies of some of our most prominent members (from past to present), to the live server. This web site is to be used as both a reference and an educational tool for students, teachers, and the general public. It was all set to

*go when I realized that one of the first comments I would get
was that the margins of the page are wider than what is
allowable for normal printing. This isn't uncommon when
designing for the web. There are typically two methods when
designing for the web. One is to use absolute widths,
specifying the specific width you want the web page to be. The
other is relative widths, which is more flexible, and adjusts to
whatever settings a user is using. At first glance, one would
assume relative widths are the better option, but some
situations dictate the use of absolute widths. Those situations
are typically when a site is graphically intensive and require
graphics to be absolutely positioned in a design. For example,
you might not want your 720 pixel wide banner to be floating
in the middle of a 100% of the screen wide design. Instead,
you create a table 720 pixels wide that contains both the
banner and the content that falls below it.*

*With wider support for CSS, and improving awareness of its
capabilities, similar placement can be accomplished without
compromising the elasticity of a design. Those using a higher
resolution can view the site the same way someone using a
lower resolution can. The benefit of going this route is that the
amount of code that you have to write can be reduced, and
that you can comply with web standards. The downside is that
it can take longer to get the results you desire.*

*I use all three approaches, and oftentimes the one I use is
dictated by what is being requested of me and how broad an
audience is. When at all possible, I try to comply with web*

standards, separating the markup from the presentation, but I don't necessarily think one way is better than the others. All have their benefits, but even striving for absolute web standardization has its pitfalls. You will find people on both sides of the fence, and I don't think there is an absolute right or wrong way.

For this specific situation, I have created a site with a minimum resolution of 800x600 in mind. As a result, what I have to do to accommodate those who might want to print out a page from the web site, is create a "printer-friendly page" option. In the past, I have done this by way of CGI scripts, but more recently by way of techniques I have learned in ColdFusion. I have to put the launch off until at least tomorrow so I can incorporate the "printer-friendly page" feature. I went ahead and created an icon resembling a printer to serve as a visual cue to the user, so all that is left is to tweak the code a bit to make it work. Looks like I'm going to have a full day tomorrow!

LESSONS/PROBLEMS

As I have said before, there aren't enough hours in a day! I have several projects to work on, but not enough time to work on them all. But that's okay; I'm happiest when I'm busy. I did get a lot done today and made some headway on improving the Education homepage, which is something I have wanted to do for some time. I didn't get to launch the biography site as I *had planned, deciding it best not to rush things and get it done right the first time. Sometimes it's very tempting to launch a site just to show it off, but why not wait for all the bells and whistles to be in place?*

PREDICTIONS

- *Work on the newsletter web site.*
- *Add "printer-friendly page" feature to biography site.*
- *Start working on design for other conference site for Stu.*
- *Read article on cross-browser compatible web site (case-study).*
- *Skim new design books purchased through Graphic Design Book Club (what a bargain!).*

DIARY

I wrapped up the biography site by adding the printer friendly feature as planned. All the script does is remove the formatting that I have placed around the content, freeing it from the wider margins, and allowing it to conform to the smaller print margins. Once I wrapped that up, I worked with Kelly to transfer the site over from the development server to the live server. I then updated the association homepage to reflect the addition of the new site. Lastly, I sent an email to staff to announce the new addition to the web site. It didn't take long before feedback started pouring in. Up to this point, it's all been positive!

I tweaked the newsletter web site further and updated a few graphics to make it more visually appealing. The editor sent me some additional revisions to the verbiage, which I took care of. I sent him another email to confirm that I had made the changes and that I would await his approval before transferring the site over to our live server.

I didn't take lunch today, as I was really busy working on these two projects, but did manage to find a little time at the end of the day to skim the new books I purchased. Unfortunately I didn't get very far, but from what I can tell they look pretty promising.

LESSONS/PROBLEMS

Today went pretty well overall. The work on the printer friendly feature took longer than I initially anticipated, but it all worked out. I was excited to finally launch the biographies site, and the initial feedback from staff was positive! Now, it's time to wait and see what the members think. I decided to skip lunch to get more done, so I left work starving! I try not to skip lunch too often, as it's nice to get a break in the middle of the day and return to my desk refreshed. On the flip side, it's sometimes better for me to simply push on, even if it means sacrificing lunch, especially when I'm in a groove.

PREDICTIONS

- Create and run WebTrends reports for committee member.
- Revise the newsletter web site further.

DIARY

Mike forwarded me an email from a committee member requesting to receive web statistics on a specific page on our web site, so that he could report the findings at an annual committee meeting. This meant that I would have to spend some time down in the server room creating and running reports to get the information he requested.

I spent several hours trying to dig up server logs from previous years, as the committee member wanted results for the current and last two years to make comparisons. Once I was able to locate the log files from the years requested, I loaded WebTrends and started to create my reports. I was going to have to run three separate reports. For the two earlier years, I had to do a little investigative work to find where the pages previously resided, as they were moved during the 2001 redesign. Once I was able to locate all of the information I needed, I ran the reports one by one. While one of the reports was running, I decided to drop in on Mike. He mentioned that he had been playing around with something that I might be interested in. It was a simple application that he coded that would allow the creation of pdf documents on the fly. This

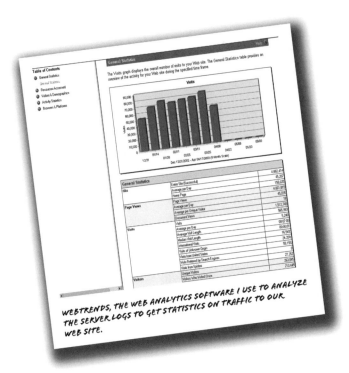

WEBTRENDS, THE WEB ANALYTICS SOFTWARE I USE TO ANALYZE
THE SERVER LOGS TO GET STATISTICS ON TRAFFIC TO OUR
WEB SITE.

could be used for numerous purposes, but what immediately
comes to mind, would be applying it to create printer-friendly
pages. In the code, you can specify what fonts should be used,
the colors, the specific location of where you want graphics
and text to be placed, and a number of other variables. He
said he was still playing around with it himself, but thought
that I might be intrigued. I told him I would take a look at it
and thanked him for the heads up.

I spent a good chunk of the day running the reports requested by the committee member and in between worked on another web site with Kelly. She was interested in knowing how I created one of my web sites I designed and how I took it from the conceptual stage to the actual code creation, so I walked her through the steps I take, by creating a dummy web page. Being a web developer, most of the work she performs is primarily on the back end, creating databases, and pages that interact with the database. My work entails everything from the interface, to interaction with the database. After walking her through the steps I typically take when creating a design, she assisted me in creating a database for the biography web site, and then tweaked the pages I created to interact more easily with the database. The results were great, and it made the site that much more self-automated and efficient.

The afternoon was pretty much a wash as we had a farewell lunch for Lisa who was departing, and after that, a small party with cake and soda. Once the events finally did wrap up, my day was through.

LESSONS/PROBLEMS
I left work with the feeling that I wasted a lot of time today. Not so much that I didn't get anything done, but it wasn't exactly how I had wanted or planned to spend my time. However, requests such as the one regarding web statistics come in from time to time, and it has to be done. I had no

problem showing Kelly my process for taking a design from conception to production, but I think I would have rather spent my time working on what I needed to get done. It was good that I was able to set up a database for the biographies web site, but I don't necessarily think that this needed to be done right away.

PREDICTIONS

- Work with Kelly on the conference web site Stu requested.
- Update the association web site to reflect the addition of the biographies site.
- Look through new books.
- Read article that I didn't get to the other day on browser/platform compatibility.

DIARY

The first thing I did this morning was update the major navigational components of the association homepage to reflect the addition of the biographies web site. Once I did that, I checked my email to answer the daily inquiries that come in from members. I looked at the reports that I ran for the committee member yesterday and compiled the results and sent them out via email. Hopefully this will cover it, as I don't particularly want to spend anymore time down in the server room running these reports!

At around 9:00, I received an email from the editor of the educational newsletter. He said he was emailing me to let me know that he was unable to view the site that I created. I tried to connect to verify the problem and realized that the development server was down. Since I am telecommuting today I wasn't able to simply go downstairs and restart the server. I had to instant message Kelly and ask her to reset the *server for me. Once that was taken care of, I let the editor know that everything was back online and that he should attempt to reconnect.*

I was hoping to get final approval on this site today so I could transfer it over to the live server and get it up and going. Unfortunately, the editor emailed me again later in the day and told me he viewed some of the pdfs of the archived issues and realized that some of the scans came out grainy and were hard to read. He said he wanted to review the other pdfs to see if there were any others that were flawed, and that he would try to address the issue prior to moving forward. He said he would get back to me sometime next week as he had a lot on his plate. I guess we'll try again next week!

After this, there seemed to be a bit of a lull in the day, so I took the opportunity to look through some Photoshop tutorials online and read some case studies on site redesigns. I'm always looking to learn new techniques and learn how others approach redesigns and other web-related issues that I encounter.

Before I called it a day, Susan called and requested to have specific pages related to our annual conference site shut off on Sunday at 5:00 p.m. These pages related to registration for the conference. The cutoff date is technically Saturday, but they usually like to allow for the stragglers to get that last-minute opportunity to get through before shutting it off completely. For the registration page itself, I entered some CFML that will check the server for the date and time, and if it

NOT HAVING A WINDOW IN MY OFFICE AT WORK, I TAKE ADVANTAGE OF HAVING A WINDOW RIGHT BESIDE MY DESK AT HOME WHEN TELECOMMUTING.

recognizes that it's Sunday, February 16 and later than 5:00p.m., it will replace what is there with a message stating that registration is closed. Unfortunately, however, the index of the web site is HTML, thus cannot utilize the CFML code. What I will need to do is log on and manually change the notice to indicate that registration is no longer open. A minor inconvenience, but won't take long to do. After I made these changes and confirmed them with Susan, I logged off for the day.

LESSONS/PROBLEMS

Today I felt I accomplished a good deal, but I didn't get as much done as I did earlier in the week. It seemed that I started out on Monday with a full head of steam and was just knocking out work left and right, but come the end of the week, things started to slow a bit. I'm in good shape, however, and the week went well overall, so I'm content. I still have not had much of an opportunity to review my new books in depth or read the article as I had intended, but I imagine I'll have some time over the weekend to catch up. I didn't get to work on the other conference site since I have to coordinate with Kelly and she was busy with some other stuff today. We will have to coordinate next week and try to get a move on as the deadline will be approaching quickly.

PREDICTIONS

- Talk to Kelly about conference web site.
- Talk to Communications about the logo and color scheme for annual conference.

DIARY

Today is my first day at work since last Thursday and it's already the middle of the week. Monday was a holiday, and Tuesday we were closed due to inclement weather. I decided to try to make it in today and had some problems with snow and ice, but did manage to eventually make it in with all limbs in tact. I can't say the same for half the staff in my building, however. A lot of people did not come in, which made it hard to get things in gear. I have a feeling that the rest of the week will be somewhat out of sync.

I spent the morning catching up on emails and reviewing submissions to the online events database. After I finished taking care of the routine tasks, I went and visited Kelly to work on the smaller conference site that we started last week. Since she wanted to take a stab at coming up with a design and going through the process I normally go through, she wanted me to give her my input on what she has thus far. After discussing what I did and did not like, we went forward with making changes to the overall aesthetics. Once we did that, we went back into the code to clean up a few minor *mistakes. Unfortunately, Mike interrupted and handed a big project to Kelly so we were unable to continue working on the site. I told her that I would continue working on it by myself and would touch base with her at a later time.*

I spent the afternoon tweaking the site further, adjusting the stylesheet, creating additional graphics, and adding a printer friendly page option to the site. It was a fairly quiet afternoon, and I made some headway, but was unable to finish the site before the day was through.

LESSONS/PROBLEMS

As I mentioned, a lot of people did not show up today including my boss, so it seemed a bit disorderly. Although I am used to working independently and have no problem doing so (as a matter of fact, I work better independently), the day did seem to drag without the interaction with other staff. I was glad we made a little progress on the conference site, but still disappointed that I didn't get to create the site myself with my ideas. Kelly took a different route, and I'm struggling to accept her final product. I think it's good to be able to teach someone how to do something she would normally not do, but at the same time I was the one initially assigned the task and I don't want it to reflect poorly on me if it is not liked or up to par with my other work.

PREDICTIONS

- Work on the smaller conference web site.
- Follow up with Communications on the color scheme and logo for the annual conference.
- Catch up with my supervisor since we haven't touched base since last week.

DIARY

I came in this morning and took care of the daily tasks before jumping into Photoshop to create an image for the opening page of the smaller conference web site. This meeting was going to be taking place in Washington, D.C., so I thought that I should create a graphic that incorporated something that someone would normally associate with the region. I decided to create a layered image that would feature both the Capitol Building and the National Monument.

I spent the morning tweaking the image, experimenting with different layer effects before getting the result I was looking for. Finally, since the web site I was creating the image for had a color scheme featuring blue, green, and yellow, I decided to give it a blue hue to blend in with the overall scheme. Once I finalized the image and incorporated it into the homepage, I sent the link to the site on the development server to Susan for review.

I decided to touch base with the Communications department regarding the logo and color scheme for our annual conference. Joan, the Communications Manager, said she would send me the logos that she had come up with thus far but said she'd like me to keep them to myself and not show anyone else for the time being. I agreed and awaited the arrival of her email. After a few minutes, her email arrived and attached was a pdf with the logos inside. The colors selected were a light shade of red and black. I reviewed the logos and sent a response with my initial feedback and a few suggestions.

Now my task will be to come up with a design for the new web site for the conference and start getting that underway. I think I like the layout that I went with this year, and though sometimes it's helpful to be consistent so that users don't have problems in transitioning from site to site each year, I think it's also good to change things up from time to time. I think the site can be used as a promotional tool, for branding purposes, and to generate some excitement for the upcoming conference. One of my biggest pet peeves is when content or designs get stale. Evolution on the web is a lot quicker than in the print world and I believe that users sometimes expect more.

LESSONS/PROBLEMS

I wrapped up the smaller conference site by completing the graphic for the homepage, and since that was my goal for the *day, I'd say I was that today was very productive. I now have the color scheme and a general idea of what the logo will look like for the 2004 annual conference, so this gives me something to work in my attempt to begin planning the design for the new site.*

PREDICTIONS

- Start working on a design for the 2004 annual conference web site.
- Look for potential training resources for creating pdfs.

DIARY

Today I worked from home, which made the week seem really short—only two days in the office! As nice as that sounds, it made getting any large projects underway difficult. With the uncertainty of everyone's schedules this week, it was also hard to get in contact with my coworkers. At any rate, today wasn't going to be much different as I had a doctor's appointment and my morning was going to be interrupted. I decided to spend the early part of the morning doing my usual morning tasks, responding to emails, and posting updates to the homepage. After I got through, 9:00 was quickly approaching and it was time to head out to my appointment.

When I returned around 11:00, I had planned on getting started on the mockups for the annual conference web site, but that plan was immediately thrown out the door when Kelly sent me an instant message shortly after I logged on. She said that Stu had reviewed the smaller conference site and that the graphic designer had made a mistake by reversing the abbreviation of one of the conference sponsors, and that he did not like the logo that he created. This meant that the logo had to be revised and re-colored. How did this affect me? Well, depending on the color selected, it could impact me a great deal or not at all. I was told to expect an email from the graphic designer with the updated logo sometime soon. The good news was that the graphic that I designed incorporating Washington, D.C. landmarks was a big hit. I was glad to hear that my biggest contribution to the project went over well.

Soon after chatting with Kelly, I received an email from a committee member that had recently requested web statistics on his committee page. He was curious why certain years had incomplete figures and wanted to know why there were some inconsistencies in the results. I was unable to figure out the exact reasoning behind the inaccuracies, but speculated that it might have to do with the fact that we installed a new web server in the last year, as well as upgraded WebTrends to a newer version. These two actions may have somehow affected the interpretation of the log files or how the log files recorded data in the first place. Although it can be frustrating when I am unable to find an answer to a question, you sometimes have to accept that you aren't always going to be able to figure things out and hope that the individual will understand. As long as you make an effort and exhaust your resources, you can take pride in knowing that you did the best that you could.

I finally received the email from the graphic designer with the updated logo and discovered that it would fit into the color scheme used on the conference site for the most part. I pulled it into Photoshop and resized it and optimized it for the web *and saved it. I then had Kelly, in addition to myself, review the site with the new logo in place. We decided that while it looked good overall, we should probably adjust the font color used on text throughout the site to match the logo color for it to look perfect. Once we adjusted the stylesheet, we ran it by Susan who gave it the final okay.*

By the time that mess was resolved it was already past lunchtime and I decided to forego eating as I wasn't very hungry and I needed to get things done. I decided to do some research for my supervisor, who had asked if I was familiar with any local resources for training in pdf creation and production. She was trying to evaluate whether or not she should send a couple of staff members to training to supplement their current knowledge of pdfs. We are using pdfs more and more for the creation of order forms, registration forms for conferences, membership forms, and for displaying our print brochures on the web. We have several staff members that have some level of expertise in pdf creation, but no one has extensive experience.

After finding some local conferences in addition to potential training options, I compiled a report with my findings along with my recommendations for what should be done. I decided that I wasn't necessarily in the position to evaluate whether or not staff should be sent for training as I didn't know what the needs were in her eyes. I wrote up some questions for her to answer for me to better evaluate the situation. I told her that I was comfortable with the level of knowledge I have in pdf creation and production for the work that I do, but depending on what is needed that might need to be reevaluated. I sent the report to her via email and will follow up with her on Monday.

As the day dwindled away, I resigned myself to the fact that I would not be drafting any designs for the 2004 annual conference web site. I did, however, receive an email from the Communications Manager with the final five logos designed for the conference taking my initial feedback into account. She took my suggestions and revised the logos to incorporate them. I thought they all looked great, but two of them really stood out. I responded to her message with my compliments and indicated which ones I thought were the best. At least I have a narrow scope for which logo I will be designing around, so I should be able to come up with something next week.

LESSONS/PROBLEMS

Another day that felt chopped up and tough to really get into anything in depth. I didn't get to start creating mockups for the annual conference web site, but it might be just as well. It's tough to start something right before a weekend and pick up right where you left off on Monday. I think it's easier to build up early in the week and just keep on rolling, so that will be my big goal for next week, barring any major interruptions.

It was frustrating to have to find out that the graphic designer made a mistake in the conference abbreviation, but it *happens. At least the mistake was caught in the production stage and not after the project went live! I was glad I was able to get my report off to my boss regarding pdf training and I think she'll be pleased with my findings/recommendations. I was also glad to receive the final logo selections from Joan for the annual conference, and even more pleased to see she took some of my suggestions into account. It's always nice to be able to contribute or assist in creating a brand. After all, this logo will be on the web site, printed materials, t-shirts, postcards, among other things! Until next week...*

PREDICTIONS

- Get started creating several mockups for the annual conference web site.
- Follow up with my supervisor on the report I compiled on potential training for staff in pdf creation and production.

DIARY

Today when I got in I was feeling pretty good, and more importantly, motivated. As mentioned on Friday, my big goal for this week was to come up with several mockups for the annual conference web site. Now that I have an idea of what the color scheme is and a narrower scope of the logo possibilities, I have a little more to go with in terms of creating a suitable web site.

I spent the entire day working on creating mockups for the new web site, only stopping to work on minor job requests as they came in. I decided that I would start out with designs that were different from what we did last year and from what we did before that. Our members aren't very receptive to change, thus feel the web site should not change very often. I agree to an extent. I understand that people are very much pattern-oriented. Once you figure something out, you go about it the way you always do, and when someone shifts or changes your pattern, you get confused or feel disoriented. On the flipside, I believe that each conference is branded to an extent, thus warranting a new look for the web site. Each year, the conference has a different color scheme, a different logo, different print promotions, so why should the web site stay the same? My plan is to carry over the major navigational elements (the major links and subheadings), while altering the aesthetics (or packaging). I think if it's done right, management should be receptive of the options I present them with. At a minimum, it will at least get them thinking for the future.

I will create at least one or two fallback designs that more closely resemble the look and feel of the site we used for this year's annual conference. This way, if things fall through, I won't have to scramble to come up with a new mockup at the last minute.

By the end of the day, I successfully created three complete mockups. All of them have somewhat similar looks in terms of their layout, but differ in how the colors are used and in the imagery incorporated into the design. I wrapped up some last minute revisions right as 3:00 arrived, and with that, I left for the day.

LESSONS/PROBLEMS

Feeling motivated when I came in this morning, I stuck to my goal for the week, which was to get started and hopefully finalize several mockups for the annual conference web site. By the end of the day, I certainly felt reaffirmed about being

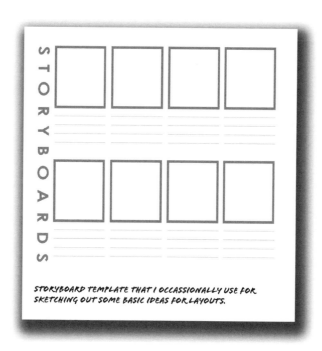

STORYBOARD TEMPLATE THAT I OCCASSIONALLY USE FOR SKETCHING OUT SOME BASIC IDEAS FOR LAYOUTS.

motivated. My plan for tomorrow is to pick up where I left off and to continue to create a few more alternative designs for the meeting committee to choose from.

PREDICTIONS

- *Finalize mockups.*
- *Create one or more mockups to add to the current selections including one that looks similar to this year's site.*

DIARY

I came in this morning still reeling from the effects of my productivity yesterday. I had several emails and a couple job requests to take care of before I could get back to the mockups for the annual conference. One of the requests that I received was to update the copyright transfer request forms for one of our publications. This merely consisted of taking MS Word documents she attached to the email and converting them to pdf and replacing what currently resides on the web. The second request was to reorganize content on the awards page, adding and removing a couple links. Again, nothing too complicated.

Once I got the job requests out of the way, I shifted my focus back to the mockups that I started working on yesterday. I went back to make some minor adjustments to a couple of the mockups and then decided to go in another direction. Working with three primary colors, I basically alternated the amount of each color and which elements were assigned the various colors to get the right balance across the various designs. The end result was a nice selection of designs for the Meetings and Events department to select from.

I focused all of my time on the mockups and spent the entire afternoon wrapping things up before calling it a day. The last thing I did before leaving was compiled a pdf of "proofs" to send to specific staff members if need be, so they can preview the designs all at once. I then printed off a copy in color for myself to reference.

LESSONS/PROBLEMS

I spent the entire day continuing my work on the mockups that I started yesterday. That doesn't leave me a great deal to write about, but hey, it's what I did! I wanted to give the Meetings and Events department a good selection to choose from and wanted to ride the creativity wave while it's here. I had a lot of ideas on how I could present the information, so I focused on coming up with as many mockups as I could from the ideas that I was visualizing in my head.

PREDICTIONS

- Possibly create one or two more mockups.
- Fix a few minor blemishes I discovered in the mockups.
- Read an article called "The 12 Deadly Sins of Site Design" that I printed yesterday.

DIARY

It was snowing again this morning, which made for a slippery commute. Nevertheless, I did manage to get in on time, but I can't say the same for the majority of the staff. It was actually a good thing as it gave an opportunity to go through a bunch of email that was awaiting me in my inbox.

I started out the day by adding information about an award to our existing listing, corrected some biographical information that appears on our new biographies web site, updated the annual conference site, adding hotel information to get ready for that to go live this weekend.

The new graphic designer, Pat, dropped by my office to ask me whether there was a simpler way to access a specific page on the annual conference web site as the full URL is very long. The graphic designers are working on both mailings and pdfs for the web and need to provide some sort of directions on how to access specific information on the web. My recommendation to him was to direct members to the annual

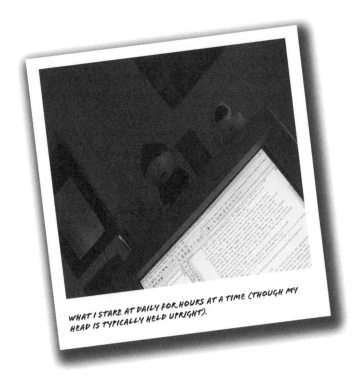

WHAT I STARE AT DAILY FOR HOURS AT A TIME (THOUGH MY HEAD IS TYPICALLY HELD UPRIGHT).

conference homepage and then click the appropriate tab on the navigation bar to reach the information they need. My opinion was that users would have trouble typing the full URL out if we printed it, and we might get a lot of phone calls. At least by sending them to the homepage, there would be a higher likelihood that they are able to figure it out for themselves as opposed to getting a 404 error (page not found). The graphic designer agreed with me and said he would let Susan know that this was how he was going to approach the dilemma.

After wrapping up the business aspect of his visit, we got a bit into web and graphic design, and we exchanged personal web sites to check out each other's work. He seemed to have more experience in the print side of graphic design, whereas my experience has primarily been in the web medium. We seemed to have some things in common, and I think we could learn a great deal from each other. I took a look at some of his work, and I noticed right away he is heavily influenced by the work he had done in print. His web sites are very graphical, which contrasts my work, which typically has more of a balanced feel. If nothing else, it was interesting to see what he can do. I'm always looking to improve on how I design, how I go about the creative process, whereas he's focused on learning more of the coding aspect and optimizing sites for the web. This was our first chance to get to know each other and I was glad we had the opportunity to talk about our experience and knowledge as we will probably work together more and more as time goes by.

Once Pat left, I went back to the mockups, fixing a few minor details that I stumbled upon last night. I also modified an existing mockup to create an alternative version. I noticed that moving one key component of the navigation changed the entire balance of the layout. I briefly ran the mockups that I had printed out by Susan to give her an idea of which direction I was going. She liked what I had to show her. I indicated that I was not entirely done yet and that not all of the designs would be submitted as choices because a few of them were merely for experimental purposes.

The day wrapped up a bit late since I had to make some last-minute revisions to the meeting site. I was in super productive mode as I wanted to get home before the roads got any worse.

LESSONS/PROBLEMS

I refined my designs a little bit more and weeded out a couple mockups from the final selection. I was able to talk at great length with the new graphic designer and it was nice to get to know him a little bit and learn about his background. Another annual conference deadline is approaching, so work is picking back up with that site. Overall, today was just an average day, but I got a lot done.

PREDICTIONS

- Read the article I keep intending to read but never get to!
- Compile the designs for the annual conference site and get ready to present them to the meeting manager in some form.
- Additional changes to the annual conference site to prepare for the impending deadline.

DIARY

Today started out like most other days, with me attending to emails and job requests that trickled in overnight. I updated a few pdf forms for the web, revised some web pages, and responded to inquiries.

Once Susan arrived, she provided me with additional information to place on the hotel and travel page of the annual conference web site. This required me to change some of the text that appeared on the page, in addition to creating graphical buttons to appear along side some of the information. She said that I would be receiving two pdfs from the Communications department that would serve as the registration forms for hotel registration at the annual conference. These forms ask for personal information of those needing rooming, in addition to specific room requests and any special requests that might be needed. They will in turn be filled out and either mailed, faxed, or emailed to association staff for processing.

While waiting for the forms to arrive, I decided to look over the mockups that I created to figure out which ones I should submit for consideration for the annual conference web site. One of the designs I came up with was much more creative than any of the others in terms of the overall layout and form of the navigation. My initial intention was to hold that one back from consideration as typically this type of design would not be one that our organization would gravitate to. However, I spoke with Kelly and she convinced me to submit it, saying that you never know what they will choose and that they could end up surprising me. With that said I decided I would go ahead and submit all seven of the mockups and any variations to Susan and the annual conference committee for review.

I made some minor touchups here and there, but overall the mockups were in good shape. I also decided that even if they weren't 100% perfect, any necessary adjustments could be made during the actual transition from mockup to working site. Now, all I need to figure out is which format I should submit the mockups in. I was thinking of simply exporting the mockups as jpegs and then creating pdfs out of the pages so that all of them would be in one large document, or alternatively putting the jpegs on the development server and providing links to each individual mockup. I'm going to think about that a little bit longer.

After lunch around noon, the pdf forms were waiting in my inbox. The only problem was that they provided me with four documents instead of the two that Susan had told me to expect. I looked at the documents and realized that they had separated the instructions from the actual registration form. I went and asked her if this was what she had intended to be done and she stated she had not and asked if I could merge the instructions with the registration form. She then said she would like to make the forms editable on the web and asked if I would be able to handle this as well. I told her that it could be done, but that it would take some time. Her goal was for everything to be finalized today, so that the hotel page could go live tomorrow.

I went back to my desk and merged the separate documents so that I was left with two instead of four. I uploaded the forms to the development server and linked to them. Now all I have to do is make them editable. I spent a great deal of time completing this task as there were 60 fields that needed to be created (from text fields to checkboxes). I then had to go back and make sure the fields worked and the text appeared correctly in the spaces provided. Lastly, I had to set the tab order for the fields so that if a user uses their tab keys they don't jump all over the document. It's not so much that it's difficult, but it can be time consuming. By 2:30, I had the forms finished and replaced what was on the web with the new versions. I emailed Susan to let her know I had finished.

She followed up by asking me if I could extract an image of a street map from one of the pdfs, in addition to providing jpegss of the registration forms themselves to provide to the hotel providing our attendees housing, so that they could place them on their own web site. I had not ever converted a pdf into an image before, but found it to be quite simple, merely having to use the "Save As" function and selecting the appropriate format. I had to go into Photoshop and crop the image a bit to get rid of excess white space, but other than that it was fairly straightforward. For the map, I simply took a screen capture of the pdf while I had it open, pulled it into Photoshop and cropped out everything but the street map and accompanying key. I saved it as a GIF and sent it on for placement on the web. After that, I left for the day.

LESSONS/PROBLEMS

I didn't get to accomplish everything that I had hoped to. I was still unable to read "The 12 Deadly Sins of Site Design," the article I printed out the other day. Nor did I get to compile the mockups for the annual conference so that they can be reviewed, but I did at least figure out what I wanted to do for the most part. I think tomorrow will be my best bet for reading the article, after I make the hotel page live and complete my routine tasks. The day was productive, but I spent a lot of time on stuff that was not anticipated (making the pdfs editable). I'm used to it at this point and for the most part have some flexibility in terms of what I am working on. If this were happening at the same time as an impending deadline, it would be a different story entirely.

PREDICTIONS

- Last-minute revisions to the hotels page of the annual conference site.
- Finally read "The 12 Deadly Sins of Site Design."
- Compile the mockups for review.

DIARY

Today was my telecommuting day and it was a good thing as we got three more inches of snow overnight with the forecast calling for several more. At least it gave me something nice to gaze at from time to time while working. I booted up my PC and logged into our intranet and had several emails waiting for me from Susan. She asked me to fix a mistake in one of the pdf registration forms, and then stated that once that I fixed the mistake that I could go ahead and make the hotel page live.

I opened up the pdf and made the correction and uploaded the new version to the development server. I then transferred over all the various components of (HTML, images, and pdfs) and the hotel page over from the development server to the live server. I checked the page to make sure all of the links and images were functional, and then placed an announcement on the homepage to indicate that this page had gone live and was accessible to the public. Everything went smoothly, and Susan met her deadline. After that, I went back and took care

THE EQUIPMENT (DSL MODEM) THAT FACILITATES MY TELECOMMUTING ONCE A WEEK FROM HOME.

of some emails that came in overnight and cleaned up my inbox a bit. I try not to let it get too cluttered or messages can get buried.

I finally had the opportunity to read the article "The 12 Deadly Sins of Site Design" published by BBC Training and Development. It was actually quite informative and more useful than I had at first anticipated. It was a case study that reviewed 12 aspects of web sites that are considered "sins of site design" and how prevalent they are in the samples they studied. It was surprising to see how many web sites still make these mistakes and how they could potentially be losing visitors because of their blunders. I think the most important "sins" outlined in this article were the overuse of unnecessary animation (annoying pop-up ads), broken or dead links, no avenue for users to contact or leave feedback, and the lack of quality of the internal search engine (if present). I think load time is still important, but not quite as high up on the list as it used to be due to the increasing amount of users obtaining Cable, DSL, etc. Even so, you don't want to overload a page with heavy graphics or big animations unless an alternative is offered to those without high-speed Internet access (and those that don't want to be bothered with anything other than text). At any rate, I thought this was a good read and had some interesting statistics.

I decided that I was going to export my mockups from Photoshop as jpegs and then simply place the screen shots in an HTML page for review. I spent the afternoon working on this, creating an aesthetically pleasing looking presentation for the screen shots. I created thumbnails for the initial page so that whoever reviews my designs gets to see them all at once and compare them side by side, and linked full-size versions if they wanted to look at any individual design more closely. I sent an email to the Susan with a link to the mockups page I created. Now it's just a matter of waiting and seeing which one gets selected. The great part about it is, whichever ones do not get selected for the final design, I can always recycle in the future. I often find myself referring back to old mockups, *pulling the best elements and applying them to new pages. So I never look at creating multiple mockups as being waste, and in fact find it to be quite beneficial.*

LESSONS/PROBLEMS

Today was productive and quiet since I worked from home. I got the hotel page launched, successfully completed the mockups for the 2004 conference meeting, created a web page to house the mockups for review and sent the link on to the Meetings and Events Manager. I was finally able to read the article, "The 12 Deadly Sins of Site Design," which I had put off several days in a row. All in all, I feel like I accomplished what I set out to do and rounded out the week quite nicely.

PREDICTIONS

- Routine tasks.
- Make sure there were no snags on the Housing & Travel page going live over the weekend.
- Look through books, clean up a little bit.

DIARY

When I got in to the office around 6:45 today, I realized that Susan was going to be out of the office on travel. This meant that the day was likely to be quiet and less stressful. This was both good and bad. Good in that it was quiet and made the environment conducive to getting a lot done. Bad in that it made the day go by slow, especially since I am waiting on her to get back to me on the mockups that I created for the annual conference.

I had a lot of email to sift through since I didn't check my email over the weekend. Normally if I'm online, I will at least check to see if any of the "die-hards" (staff that seem to eat, breathe, and sleep work) have sent me emails after business hours. This weekend, however, the mail server was being taken offline to undergo a major upgrade.

In the midst of going through my inbox, Tanya, the Meetings and Events Assistant came into my office and told me that there was information that they had neglected to provide me to place on the conference web site. While we had provided instructions and a link to the hotel reservation web site, we did not instruct users as to what source code they would need to provide while filling out their reservation requests. Luckily, we had not received any questions as of yet; however, if anyone already made their reservations, they could be out of luck as the hotel will have no way to tie their reservation to our event and room block! At any rate, I was able to craft a brief blurb about the source code and made it prominent enough so that it would not be missed.

After that fire was put out, I moved on to an email from the editor of the educational newsletter that I recently had been creating a web site for. He had revised all of the content and asked that I update the site to reflect this as soon as possible. Lucky for him I had nothing major on my plate today, so I made the changes right away and sent him a confirmation once completed. Several other smaller updates were waiting for me, so I wiped them out and responded as necessary.

Right before I went to lunch, I received a solicitation for a workshop that was being offered in August. Normally I do not submit the events to the online event database myself because we also print the information in our membership magazine, and most times I'm not able to fill in the missing data (such as in this case), should they not provide complete information. However, from time to time you receive an event in printed form and to go back and track down where the solicitation originated is almost more trouble than entering the

MY FILING CABINET WHERE I STORE JOB REQUESTS FOR UP TO A YEAR AFTER THEIR COMPLETION.

information yourself. So I went through the process of submitting the event and then approving it on the administrative end.

When I returned from lunch around 1:00, I decided that I should spend some time cleaning up files on my computer. When I am juggling multiple projects at once, my desktop and project directories tend to get cluttered. From source files to full working prototypes, things can get pretty messy after a while. I tried to get rid of files that I no longer needed and anything that I thought I could have used in the future I tried to archive in a single directory. I also tried to clean up my file cabinet by getting rid of anything that I no long need. I keep all job requests submitted to me in my desk for three months before moving them to my filing cabinet, where they will remain for nine months. After a year has transpired, I dispose of the old requests. The reason I keep them for a year is that oftentimes people submit a request and return at a later time asking why such and such was done, or come back in a few months and forget how they went about a certain process. Unfortunately, my brain can only absorb so much information and despite what my coworkers seem to think, I don't remember every single request that is submitted to me. I complete a request, and move on to the next. Granted if it's a large project, I'm likely to remember, but there are a lot of smaller and more obscure requests that come with the territory and remembering them all is impossible.

At the end of the day I had a little free time, so I decided to look through the books that I purchased a while back. I'm always scanning, observing, and taking in what I see. This is how I generate new ideas, and find the motivation I need to keep creating. I'd almost go so far as to say it's a workout of the mind. I'm always looking for inspiration, a new approach, and the next project. I'm looking for ways to improve and ways to top previous accomplishments.

Right before I left for the day I received a response from the newsletter editor stating that he was very pleased with my work and that I had been a pleasure to work with. His appointment as editor for the journal is coming to an end and his final goal during his tenure was to have a new web site created and launched for the newsletter. With my help, it went from a goal to a reality, and quickly. The site is a major improvement both in functionality and aesthetics. It was really nice to receive praise and it felt good that I was able to help someone else. Ending the day on a good note is certainly the way to go!

LESSONS/PROBLEMS

Today seemed slower than usual, and I did not receive an overabundant amount of requests. I finished what I needed to and made great strides in getting the newsletter web site ready to launch. I think I might start brainstorming another long-term project that I can keep myself busy with during the downtimes. I don't think I could really take on anything too extensive as things will be picking up again as begin to get closer to the annual conference (July). People seem to start crawling out of the woodwork as it gets closer to the conference and when they need to report on their accomplishments, and this means more work for me. It's nice that they have someone so dependable, efficient, and fast onboard to cover their backs!

PREDICTIONS

- Follow up with Susan about the hotel page.
- Talk to Susan about the mockups for the conference site.

DIARY

This morning seemed to pick up where yesterday left off. I didn't have a whole lot of requests waiting for me, and I have no major projects to work on at the moment. Everything seems to be in a hold pattern, which can be frustrating. After my usual routine, I followed up with the editor of the newsletter to let him know that I appreciated his positive feedback and to confirm that I would be transferring over the web site as soon as I received the okay from the director on our end.

Apparently someone from one of our sister organizations accused us of being in violation of their "fair use policy" in regard to our use of their logo. The educational newsletter has been published jointly for 20 years and has always incorporated their logo. Your guess is as good as mine as to why it is an issue now. At any rate, Dave reassured me that it was a misunderstanding and that he would iron it out. We received word today from the sister organization that we need to abide by their "fair use policy" and can only use the logo that they provide us with and must maintain the dimensions in which it was created. I have not had a chance to check out the logo yet, but I will need to replace what is currently on the new web site with the one they send us and then get their approval prior to making the web site live. Either they were unaware for the last 20 years that they were jointly publishing this newsletter with their logo on it, or someone decided to tighten the noose in regards to copyright issues and is going off the deep end. Oh well, just another day in the life…

After my midday lunch, I decided to check in with Susan on the status of the mockups and she stated that she hadn't had a chance to look at them because she was still playing catch up. She said that she would get back to me later. I had a feeling that this would be the case, but I try to make sure I'm on top of things so nothing slips through the cracks.

Since, for the second day in a row I was left with some free time, I decided to peruse our web site to look for outdated content and rotate the news and announcements on the homepage to freshen things up a bit. I checked on the biographies web site that we recently launched and everything looked okay. I am actually surprised that I have heard very little in terms of feedback from anyone. From my experience here, though, no feedback is generally a good sign as our members tend to only speak up when they are either confused, experiencing problems, or have distaste for something. This is not always the case, but the majority of feedback occurs when something is not working. I'm hoping that once the site is advertised in our membership magazine, more people will be aware of this tool and will give us feedback and hopefully contribute to what we already have. The day ended the same way it started, with a whisper.

LESSONS/PROBLEMS

I did not expect today to be quite as slow as yesterday, but apparently I was wrong. I'm going to have to brainstorm a little bit more and work on coming up with some long-term projects to work on when things get slow or when projects are on hold for other people. On the other hand, it is nice to have a little down time to catch up on tasks that you might otherwise neglect.

PREDICTIONS

- Brainstorm to come up with some long-term projects.
- Evaluate whether or not it would be worth pursuing training on any specific area/skill/language.
- Test software programs.

DIARY

Happy hump day! It's Wednesday, the middle of the week, the halfway mark. Not that I'm keeping track or anything. I decided that since it was the first week of the month, I would go downstairs to the server room and run a couple WebTrends reports to update the latest web statistics for the staff that request them. It is something that can be automated, but I only recently transferred the software over from our development server to our live server, which is the lifeline of our web and database operations. If WebTrends were to lock up the system, it would be a big problem. I wouldn't be as concerned if it had not caused problems in the past on the development server. Of course, a lot of it probably had to do with the fact that there was not much in the way of disk space or memory available for indexing, which can consume a great deal of both. At any rate, I like to play it safe and run the reports manually so I can monitor their progress.

Once the reports finished running, I went back upstairs to my office to sift through my email. I received word from one of the director's that he had received an email from our sister organization with their "Terms of Use" and two versions of their logo attached.

After reviewing the "Terms of Use," I grew a bit frustrated because I was getting the feeling that they were being overly restrictive about the use of their logo and I couldn't figure out why. Perhaps they recently had some problems with people publishing an altered logo, or had something attributed to them that was not technically theirs. From my experience, organizations are usually pretty flexible so long as what you use resembles their original logo. This organization gave specifics, from the colors that can be used, to dimensions and size, and even space that must be allotted on all sides of the logo. I spoke with the Education Manager about the issue and she mentioned that they attended a meeting she was at this weekend and the logo issue came up and became quite a heated discussion. Apparently they were quite distressed by its use, but it was not clear as to why. She said she was almost getting the impression that they were simply looking for an excuse to terminate our partnership. Sometimes I guess it's just best to jump through hoops to preserve long-term relationships.

I pulled the header image that I created for the newsletter web site into Photoshop and modified it to reflect the requirements of the sister organization. It took a while because of how I altered the logo to blend it into the graphic I had created. But now, due to their restrictions, I had to tweak my initial design.

Once I finished experimenting with different looks, I finalized the image, sliced it up, and exported it directly into the images directory. I uploaded the new header to the development server and let the director know so he could have our sister organization verify that what I had done was acceptable.

It dawned upon me that Stu had mentioned at a recent staff meeting that he wanted to have all staff send him an email outlining any and all training, reading, or professional development that we had done in the last year. The reason he did this was that he thought it would be useful for the Board of Directors to hear when working on the bonus package for the upcoming year. He said that this would not serve as an evaluation tool but thought it would be beneficial for the board to know since we don't necessarily work with them on a regular basis. I decided to type up a Word document listing all of the books that I had purchased in the last year or so, both through work and on my own, related magazine subscriptions, web sites that I routinely visit for industry news and developments, tutorials that I have experimented with, and my professional memberships. When I finished, I was actually surprised with all that I had done in the last year. I definitely feel that I am pretty progressive in my pursuit of personal growth and am motivated to stay current as the field that I work in is always evolving, and evolving quickly.

In the afternoon, I updated some pdf forms on the web to reflect new prices. Then, I sent the vendor who maintains our electronic publications web site an email to have them revise some verbiage on the homepage. Before I left for the day, I stopped in the Susan's office and she showed me the three logos that the annual conference committee had selected as their favorites. Sure enough, my favorite (and the one I used in my mockup designs) was among that group. She explained the reasoning behind their choices and seemed to agree with me that the one I selected was the best. Unfortunately it's not our decision, but with any luck they'll choose the "right one."

LESSONS/PROBLEMS

Progress was made in getting the web site finalized for the educational newsletter. Hearing back from our sister organization was a step in the right direction. It enabled me to alter the header as needed to comply with their "Terms of Use." All that is left is for them to give us the final okay and it can be put to rest. I sent Stu an outline of all of the training, books, and professional development that I received or participated in during the last year so that he can assure the Board of Directors that association staff are staying current and continuing to develop their skills and enhance their knowledge. All in all, it was nice to make some progress and attend to things that I had previously put on the back burner.

PREDICTIONS

- Transfer over the educational newsletter web site to the live server.
- All-Staff Meeting.

DIARY

An ugly, dreary, wet day; it was hard to get motivated to come in today. The weather aside, today is our monthly staff meeting and it is going to be tough to keep myself from falling asleep. Actually, it's not really that bad anymore. Our meetings used to last two and a half hours, but they have been cut back to roughly an hour. Instead of going around the room having each person say what they have been working on over the last month (taking turns boring each other), we now only make announcements that impact all staff. It certainly makes it easier to pay attention and is not as much of an inconvenience.

The meeting ended after lasting just over an hour. Nothing too extraordinary transpired, but I did learn that we would be getting a new Assistant Director starting in October. The Assistant Director will serve as my boss's supervisor, just under the Executive Director. She will be overseeing both the Publications and Education departments (with most of the focus being on improving Education). When she comes aboard, she will focus on bringing another staff member aboard to

WHENEVER I DO DECIDE TO LEAVE, MY SUCCESSOR WILL HAVE A LOT OF DOCUMENTATION TO REFER TO.

work under her and along side the current Education Department staff members.

When I got back to my desk, I received an email from Dave stating that our sister organization had approved the use of their logo on the newsletter web site. Finally, I was given the greenlight to go ahead and make the new site live. I pulled up ColdFusion, dragged the entire directory over from the development server to the live server, and was done! I pulled up the site in a web browser and tested the links and *navigation to make sure everything was working as it should. After giving it a quick run through, I sent an email to the Communications Manager, Education Manager, Publications Manager, and the editor of the newsletter to inform them all that the site was complete and now live. Another project crossed off the list!*

I decided to order lunch out since it was so nasty outside. After I finished eating, I ran into the Communications Manager on my way back to my office. She said she really liked the design that I created for the newsletter site and that she would love to use the color scheme for an association site redesign and for new business cards and letterhead. I of course would love to do a redesign and think it would be great if we could coordinate a redesign of our print and web materials to coincide with the opening of our new building. It would generate some excitement for staff and would give us an opportunity to do what we do best, all the while modernizing and freshening up our look! She said that she would work on coming up with a proposal even though she fears we might meet resistance. I told her I would be more than happy to assist and that I thought it would be a great idea. This could potentially be the long-term project that I have been looking for.

Before I knew it, the day's end had arrived. I spent the rest of the afternoon reviewing documentation, getting rid of items that are no longer relevant, updating others where necessary. It was neat to see some of the emails and notes that were saved from when I first started working here and realizing how far we have come since that time. It seems that we have more direction now than we did then, have more consistency, and are certainly a lot more organized and efficient. Anyhow, I know how disoriented one can be when they start a new job, and having some sort of historical reference can be quite beneficial when trying to understand why we did what we did. This is why I have created a binder with notes, correspondence, and other related materials for my future replacement and anyone else who might be interested down the line.

LESSONS/PROBLEMS

The morning was broken up due to the staff meeting, which made it difficult to really get anything going early on in the day. However, I was finally able to make the newsletter site live, which brought another project to conclusion. My other big accomplishment for the day was that I cleaned up and added new content to my documentation binder, which will be useful for anyone who wants to know the history of web-related decisions at the association.

PREDICTIONS

- Check on status of membership marketing campaign.
- Clean up and organize home PC.
- Read/peruse Photoshop book.

DIARY

Ah yes, nothing like waking up at 6:45 in the morning wishing I could roll over and go back to sleep, only to realize that "hey, at least it's my telecommuting day and I don't have to physically leave my apartment." I rolled out of bed, threw some water on my face, put on some coffee, and booted up my computer. I turned on the TV for some background noise, opened the blinds, and plopped down in my computer chair.

I anticipated the day being a pretty quiet one since a lot of people schedule their telecommuting day on Fridays. As a result, there are only a few people actually in the office and it is usually pretty laid back. When I am bombarded with work on a Friday, it's typically something given to me from the Meetings and Events department, or a request that comes in from an outside source (not from staff). I wasn't expecting to receive anything, but one never knows with them. From what I can tell, however, today is going to be one of the more low-key days.

Some time ago, I participated in a series of meetings with Gina, Dave, Mike, and Kelly. The purpose of the meetings was to brainstorm and come up with ways of marketing our membership to potential members. Basically, when one obtains membership, they receive certain benefits, but we do not do a good job of centralizing those benefits to actually look like something tangible to users. Under our "Members Only" section of the web site, the only option available to members is the ability to update their personal information. Some benefit, huh? Well, if you were a member and you saw this, you might begin to wonder what the heck you were paying for!

We met to discuss what benefits we do offer and come up with a way to centralize these items in one location that we could send members to once they joined. This would serve as the new "Members Only" or "Membership" web page. The web page itself will be accessible to both members and non-members, allowing non-members to see what the benefits of membership are, all the while centralizing the information for current members to facilitate navigation. My job was to come up with a catchy design for this web page that looked different from the rest of our web site and present the content in an organized manner. Gina's task was to identify the content, while Mike and Kelly were to assist me in linking up the portions that were only accessible via member log-in, and Dave was overseeing the whole project.

I created several mockups for the project, using the information provided to me by Gina. I tried to go for a modern look, incorporating images of professionals and building off of a theme of "what can we do for you?" Each benefit listed was *given its own page, with a description of the benefit and a link to relevant information. When I completed the mockups, everyone voted on their favorite, and then I worked on converting it over to HTML. After I did that, I informed the group that I completed the web page and asked them to let me know what the next step was.*

It has been several months since that time and nothing has been done to move this project forward. I decided to inquire by sending Gina an email asking if this project was going to be moving forward soon or if it had been scrapped. As I had suspected, the project had been placed on the back burner, in favor of more urgent matters. It was good that I inquired, though, as Gina then met with Dave about it, who said that we would definitely be pushing forward with this project hopefully sometime around April. Gina followed up with an email to me stating that she really thought this was an important project and that she would be content on working on it with me alone, so that we would have something in final form to present in April. That way, the Membership Committee will be more likely to address it and less likely to put it on the back burner again. I was relieved to hear that they still thought this was important, as I certainly do. I plan to follow up with her again sometime soon to start hammering out the details as to where we need to go with it to get it in shape to roll it out.

After going back and forth about that issue, I decided to shift my attention and try to clean up my computer a little bit.

Much like my work computer, my home computer has become quite cluttered, and there are files and directories scattered throughout. I decided to go through each directory to see what was in them and decide whether or not the files needed to be saved for future use or if they were disposable. I was surprised at how much had built up in the last six or so months of telecommuting on Fridays and how many different versions of the same files there were due to the various revisions and updates that had been made in that time. I saved all of my source files, got rid of a lot of duplicate files, and created project-based directories to store essential components of those projects.

Lunch for the day was a can of tuna fish without mayonnaise. I was starting to regret having telecommuted today. Then again, if I had anticipated and thought about purchasing lunch food when I went grocery shopping last weekend, I might actually have something more exciting available to me! Although not very inspiring, I felt refreshed, so I guess it served its purpose.

As I had suspected it would be, the day had been pretty quiet. I had not received a single phone call, and very few, if any emails trickled in to my inbox. It was almost too quiet. Oh well, it certainly made the environment more conducive to getting other things accomplished. I decided to spend the afternoon looking through the latest issue of Photoshop User, the membership magazine published by the National Association of Photoshop Professionals (NAPP) and to continue looking through my book, "Adobe Photoshop 7 Web Design with GoLive 6" by Michael Baumgardt.

I love Photoshop User and would gladly pay the amount I paid for NAPP membership just for the magazine alone if I had to (the subscription comes as a benefit of NAPP membership). There are so many cool Photoshop tutorials that show you how to incorporate the most current and trendy techniques in design into your work, as well as questions and answers, product, software, and book reviews, among other things.

After looking through the latest issue of Photoshop User, I moved on to the Photoshop book, which also had some great examples of techniques and how to apply them to web design. The book provides examples of completed projects in addition to complete walk-throughs on how to accomplish different effects. Most importantly, it provides a great deal of information on how to combine the power of Photoshop and GoLive to best optimize your creations for use on the web.

By the end of the day, I had successfully practiced some of the techniques shown in both the magazine and book. I checked my email once again just to make sure I didn't have anything urgent waiting for me, but there were no messages. I decided to call it a day so I logged off and shut down my computer.

LESSONS/PROBLEMS

I had a chance to clean up a little bit, look through a couple publications, and inquire about a project that was placed on the back burner some time ago. It was nice to get some low-priority things accomplished, and to have a day where the pace was set by me and not by the work that I was assigned.

PREDICTIONS

- *Plan for potential future redesign.*
- *Routine tasks.*
- *Turn in timesheet.*

DIARY

Monday morning. When I got in, I had a request in my inbox from Mara asking me to review the budget figures from last year and to start figuring out what I wanted to request for the next year. This included everything from office supplies, dues and subscriptions, to software support. I decided that this would be the first thing I would focus on today since it was important and time sensitive.

I felt the best way for me to figure out what I would request for the upcoming year would be to try to identify what items would be recurring in the upcoming year. Mara gave me a printout that showed what was allotted for various purposes for and what was spent to date. This helped refresh my memory as to what types of expenses I incurred in the last year, which assisted in my planning for the upcoming year. Most of the money that I use is put toward membership dues (NAPP, IWA), subscriptions, and training. Most of my software and hardware support is handled through the IT manager, so outside of money for dues and general office supplies, I'm pretty much set. I enjoy having the ability to submit a budget proposal as it has given me a better understanding of the process and has helped me in planning and identifying what the typical expenses are working as a web designer, on an annual basis.

Once I finished typing up my budget proposal, I printed it out and turned it in to Mara. She was quite surprised when I told her I was finished. What she had failed to tell me when she gave me last year's figures was that I had a month to get back to her with my proposal! Actually, I most likely would have hammered it out right away anyhow, since I don't like to sit on stuff of this nature. It's good to strike while the iron is hot and when things are slower than usual. If I had waited on it, I am certain things would have gotten busy and then I would be rushing to get things finished at the last minute. Finally, it gives my boss one less thing to worry about.

Later on I received an email request from a member of one of our regional chapters. He contacted me to let me know that the URL to their homepage had changed and that it needed to be updated on our chapter's homepage. He also asked if I knew of a way that he could make it so that if anyone went to the old homepage that they could automatically be redirected to the new location. Finally, his last question was about having a mailing list set up for his chapter. I first forwarded the message on to Kelly since the link that appears on the chapters homepage is actually stored in a database that she maintains. After I passed that piece on to her to handle, I responded to the member to let him know that the URL had been changed on our end and gave him simple instructions on how to set up a simple HTTP redirect in the old homepage so users would not get lost in the move. Lastly, I outlined the steps that needed to be taken to have a message list set up for his chapter.

After lunch, Joan visited my office and told me which logo of the final three the 2004 conference committee selected. Unfortunately, it wasn't the one that I had hoped would be picked. I feel that I have a pretty good overall design sense and when given a selection of images to select from, there are typically one or two that stand out above the rest for various reasons. I had three favorites and two of them made it to the final round of voting by the conference committee. In the grand scheme of things it is not that big of a deal, but I think my top selection would have had the perfect balance of color and would have been the best in terms of branding the conference. I guess it's up to me to make the logo shine once the committee makes a decision on which layout they prefer for the web site. The bad news is that there are a few layouts that I feel stand out above the rest, and I'm not sure (judging by previous decisions) the committee will make the "right choice"! To be honest, whichever design they do select will work fine for me. Typically, the final design gets polished and often ends up better than the mockup itself, so everything should work out great in the end.

I spent the tail end of my day coming up with some mockups for a new homepage for the association should I be given the opportunity to redesign the site in the not too distant future. I was feeling motivated after Joan's recent comments about the possibility of a redesign stemming from the web site I created for the educational newsletter. Going with a similar color scheme, I started to play around with a few ideas and tried to get some of my thoughts out on the canvas. I think it's always good to tap into whatever energy you have when it's there in terms of creativity. You never know when you'll hit a rut, and in this case, you never know when you'll need a layout or have to redesign the web site. It felt good to start thinking about the possibilities and experiment a little bit.

LESSONS/PROBLEMS

I worked on and submitted my budget proposal. The logo selection for the annual conference was made and I was somewhat disappointed with their selection. To be honest, I was also sort of surprised. I really felt passionate about one of the logos and hoped that it would be the clear standout. In fact, I used it in all of the mockups that I created for the web site. Maybe they'll change their mind after they see what I did with my favorite! The lesson of the day? Everyone sees things differently. I still say analytical people should not be making decisions on aesthetics, but that's just my two cents! But seeing as how we are here for the members and the conference committee consists of members, giving them what they want is most important.

PREDICTIONS

- Continue experimenting and creating designs for future use.

DIARY

It's 7:15 am, Tuesday morning. I'm awake, I'm energized, I have my coffee, and I am ready to work. While booting up, I wolfed down my sandwich bag of dry cereal and washed it down with a swig of freshly brewed Dunkin Donuts coffee. Ah, yes, this is the life. Now I'm ready to roll.

Before I even managed to check my email, Susan came into my office and asked if I could make a change to a form for her. Sound vague? It did to me, too. After going back and forth prodding for more specifics, I finally realized she wanted me to revise the hotel form that I had created in pdf format for the annual conference. Apparently, she indicated for one of the hotels, that they had an option to stay in a room with two double beds, while the hotel in fact doesn't offer that option at all! The other mistake was that people were given the option to stay in a non-smoking room when the entire hotel is a non-smoking facility. Not a major problem, but kind of funny. My guess is that the only reason it was discovered is because one of our members actually submitted a hotel form with these options selected and the hotel was probably raising their eyebrows wondering what was going on. The good news is that these mistakes were caught early on in the process, and if there were ever a good time to catch these kinds of mistakes, it would definitely be now. I pulled the pdf form up in Adobe Acrobat and simply deleted these two options and replaced them with a statement that said that the hotel was a smoke-free facility. That should clear up any confusion. Once I completed the revisions, I let Susan know that everything was taken care of.

With a caffeine buzz starting to kick in, I opened up Outlook and deleted the usual 20 some odd junk emails I get on a daily basis (if I only had a penny for every Nigerian money scheme email I receive…). Finally, a work-related email worked its way to the surface. It was from Tina, the Special Projects Assistant who typically handles our elections and board-related matters. She was contacting me to let me know that the vendor for online elections had provided her with a link to the electronic ballot and wanted to inform me that members could start voting as soon as they received their ballot package in the mail. She asked me to post an announcement on the homepage along with a catchy graphic to draw people's attention to it.

This was of particular interest to me since I served on a Process Improvement Team several months ago that looked into the feasibility of the association providing the option of online voting for our annual election to members. After doing extensive research, talking to several vendors, and benchmarking other organizations, we compiled our findings with our recommendations (in favor of providing the option of

MY DAILY MORNING CAFFEINE FIX.

online voting) and presented them to Stu. He in turn presented it to the Board of Directors who approved the motion. The only stipulation was that for the first year, we provide the option of online voting or paper ballots. We could then phase out the paper ballots over time (once members become more comfortable and familiar with the online environment). This was the first I had heard anything since I got word that we would be moving forward with online voting. It's pretty cool to know that I had an influence on a decision such as this. Seeing *it play out before my eyes is pretty inspiring. I'm doubly pleased since it's a push to get people to venture out online. We have a lot of members who don't like change and who seem to have a fear of the Internet. Perhaps something as important as this might get members who otherwise might not, to take that step into the virtual jungle that is the Internet.*

I decided that I would create an animated graphic to go along with the announcement about the start of annual election and the new ability to submit ballots online. I played around with a few ideas in Imageready before figuring out what I wanted to do. I decided I'd create a simple graphic that consisted of text that said "VOTE HERE!" and an empty checkbox. The animation aspect of the graphic would be the check appearing in the checkbox. It would materialize as it would if it were being written by hand. I worked on the animation until shortly before lunch, at which time I placed it along side of the announcement, and put it on the development server for review by the Tina. I fired off an email to let her know that I had finished her request and asked her to review what I had done and to let me know if and when she wanted it to go live. After that, I peeled myself away from my desk to go out for a brisk walk to get some grub.

When I returned from lunch at about 1:00, I had received a response from Tina, and she was really pleased and impressed with the animated graphic I created. She asked if I could possibly incorporate one more item into the announcement, but once that was done it had her approval. The unfortunate thing was that she wanted an item incorporated that wasn't on the web yet. It was an article written by the association president related to voting that is supposed to appear in the membership magazine that I post online each month. I had not received the article from Communications yet, so I went and obtained it, along with the other monthly teasers I put up to advertise our membership magazine. I spent the rest of the afternoon working on getting the teasers ready to go, resizing and optimizing the magazine cover image, creating the table of contents, and formatting the articles for the web, testing them out on the development server, and finally making everything live. Once that portion was taken care of, I was finally able to make the election announcement live. I sent out one final email to let all parties involved that the election announcement was made public and that the president's letter was up as well.

LESSONS/PROBLEMS

I had a good day. I received a request that reminded me of how important my contributions are to the organization. It also gave me an opportunity to create an animated graphic (although not specifically requested), which was a nice change since I don't get to do them as regularly as static graphics.

PREDICTIONS

- Review calendar for expiring web pages.
- File job requests from December through February.
- Pick up a copy of the final presented paper compilation on CD.
- Look through latest issue of membership magazine.
- Continue working on designs for future use.

DIARY

I woke up at 5:45 a.m. feeling like I hadn't slept a wink. Regardless, I dragged myself out of bed, showered and got ready for work. After showering in semi-scalding water for about five minutes, I was able to wake myself up a little bit before heading out to work. I grabbed my snacks for the day and took off out the door. At this point, everything was going as planned. Not for long! When I approached my car, I noticed something didn't look right. Apparently, someone decided (at random) to splatter a few eggs on my car. Beautiful! To make matters worse, the temperatures are still pretty cold here, so the mess was frozen and harder to remove from the car. The only good thing was that I didn't have to contend with the gooey yolk, since it was more or less solidified. I guess that's the price I pay for driving a sports car. It certainly could have been worse! At any rate, this delayed my arrival at work by a good half-hour, as I got stuck in the morning rush.

UGH, TIME TO GET UP!

When I got in at around 7:30, I immediately fired off an email to the leasing office of my apartment complex to inform them of the egging. I thought they should be made aware since they recently sent out a notice that another resident's car had been broken into. They supposedly have a courtesy officer that patrols the complex, but to this date I have never seen anyone, but who knows, maybe this will increase the frequency of their patrolling.

I went about my morning as I usually do, picking up my mail, checking my email, and reviewing submissions to the online events database. The only request I received overnight was to post an announcement on the homepage regarding an impending deadline for a research opportunity. I went ahead and took care of that request, signing off on it and filing it away.

I then went into my calendar to look for any expiring web pages and removed them from the web. On my job request form, I provide a field for staff to provide an expiration date for content. This wasn't done until I started working here, which allowed for a lot of stale and outdated content to remain up on the web. While in some cases it is intentional, we currently have over 3,000 pages, and I don't think we should clutter up the server any more than we need to. Besides, who wants to look at an announcement for a job opening from two years ago?

At around 11:00, I went down to the first floor to grab the latest issue of our membership magazine, and a copy of the compilation of papers that were presented at last year's conference on CD to review. I always make a point to look at the latest issue of our membership magazine to make sure I'm up to date on member-related issues and organization-wide news. This helps me field the various phone and email inquiries I receive on a variety of issues. As for the CD? Well, since I had such a big role in its organization and in the decision making last year, helped manage the web site for paper submission this year, and consulted on other related issues, I'm always interested to see how the final product turns out. Last year we had a crisis due to a mistake made on the vendor's part, which required them to reproduce all 2,500 CDs and send out a second shipment to those who ordered them. Needless to say, this wasn't a good way to introduce a new product to our membership, and some members were pretty critical in their feedback. This year, the web interface was greatly improved and much more user friendly. Having already tested a beta copy of the CD, I think the same can be said about it too this time around. I feel last year was a learning experience and this year's process and overall product are much improved. The membership will hopefully be pleased with the results.

At 12:00, I was feeling pretty hungry and decided to go grab a bite to eat from the deli around the block. I came back and finished looking at the March issue of our membership magazine. A lot of the information that appears in the magazine gets filtered to me for placement on the web, but not everything. When I was finished perusing the magazine, I decided to give the CD a whirl. I pulled it out of the slick CD cover that accompanies it branded with last year's conference logo. I popped it in and immediately a splash screen popped up that incorporated the same logo along side of the menu for navigating the CD. I decided to look at some of the papers, which are stored in pdf format and was impressed. A lot of the papers contain tables and graphs and the ability to maintain their integrity is important to both the viewer and the authors of the papers. I tested the various search funtions (keyword, author, paper title, free-text) to see how well they functioned,

TODAY WAS JUST ONE OF THOSE DAYS.

and again was impressed. One of the new features that we added was the program book from the conference so that users could look through it as they would the print version (by day), and click on what they wanted to see from that day. This was something that was requested by the members, and it's a definite enhancement to what we had last year. Not too shabby! It should be interesting to see what the various committees and member representatives have to say when I attend their meetings at this year's annual conference.

By 1:30, I had exhausted my interest in perusing the CD and my efforts to try and break it using the various features it *presented me with. I decided it was time to move on to Photoshop to experiment with designs again. I turned off my overhead lights, and instead turned on a smaller and less intense lamp that I like to use when working long hours (and designing) on the computer. It's a lot easier on the eyes and helps keep the temperature down (it gets hot up here on the top floor!).*

With this new design, I am shifting the color scheme from warmer colors to cooler colors, which consist of several hues of blue. If this design is ever approved for use by our organization, it would be quite a transition in terms the overall feel of the site simply due to the shift in colors. The navigation and header image will function as they typically would but will also assist in framing in the "guts" or main content. This will help the user from getting distracted and at the same time give them the ability to navigate throughout the site at any point without drawing them away from what they are looking at.

Around 2:30, I had made a considerable amount of progress with the design, until the unexpected occurred. Adobe Photoshop crashed and threw out three quarters of the changes that I had made to the mockup! Talk about frustrating. I'm usually good about saving as I go along, but when I start using layer upon layer upon layer, it takes longer to save each time. Luckily for me this wasn't a project that was assigned to me with a deadline or else I'd really be upset. Instead, I tried to look at it as a minor setback, as I can always recreate what was lost. But not today.

Taking the crash as a sign, I decided not to attempt to work on the design any further. A couple staff members had dropped off requests for me to take care of, so I chose to knock those out before heading out for the day. One was simply placing an announcement about a member who recently received an award for his profound contributions to the scientific field. The other request was a follow-up to one that had been submitted previously. Apparently after reviewing my initial changes, the requester decided that a few more minor adjustments needed to made to the web site before she would be content. Following the completion of the requests, I signed off on them, and filed them away and let the requesters know of their completion.

On my way out, I ran into Susan and she inquired about the annual conference web site design. Apparently she was under the impression that I had selected a final design and had begun working on the actual coding of the web site, when in fact her intial request was for me to create the designs and submit them to her for review. She confessed that she had not read my email with the link to the seven options available to her. She said that she normally chooses the design herself and then shows the conference committee the final design. I told her that was fine, and that I had one or two designs that I preferred over the rest and would be happy to simply choose my favorite and get underway with the construction of the web site. She said that she would read my email and review the designs I submitted to her and then we could meet to decide on which one we should move forward with. I agreed and we parted ways. As you can see, there is always room for improvement when it comes to communication. Sometimes you find out you have more leeway than you thought at the onset. Great, I love to call the shots. Consider me delighted.

LESSONS/PROBLEMS

Lesson one for the day: SAVE OFTEN. Adobe Photoshop crashed on me, and I lost 75% of the changes that I made when working on the mockup for a future redesign. I lucked out in that it wasn't something that I was assigned to do, but it still stinks. Lesson two: Communication is the key! Sometimes people try to fill in the blanks when they don't have all of the necessary information and it works, but other times it doesn't. So if you aren't sure about something, inquire, ask, and solicit input. No question is a stupid question. It's better to know too much than not enough. Lesson three: Output is a direct result of what is input. If you give 100% of yourself, you should have favorable results. Finally, lesson four: Expect the unexpected. Nothing in this world is certain.

WHERE I'M GOING NEXT

It's great waking up each morning knowing that no matter what transpires during the day ahead, nothing can discount that I am doing what I love. I have been given the opportunity to use my creativity and passion for design, to create tools and applications that are helping 15,000 people from all around the world further their knowledge and experience in a field that they are passionate about. On top of that, I get paid for it! It certainly makes going to work a much more rewarding experience. Not everyone can say that they love what they do and do what they love.

Though I have been working for the association for four and a half years, I know that there may come a time that I decide to move on and continue on my journey. I plan to continue working in the design field regardless, further developing my knowledge and experience in all facets of design. Using my creative instincts, I will work toward effective solutions to whatever projects are presented to me. My long-term goal is to get to a level of knowledge and security that will provide me the opportunity and flexibility to start my own consulting business.

AT MY DESK

I approach my career ambitions as I do my life. If you make the most of every day, and put forth your best effort, things will take care of themselves. There will always be unavoidable and unexpected setbacks, and sometimes risks, but how you react to them makes all the difference. If you approach setbacks as learning opportunities, and criticism as constructive feedback, you can accomplish anything.

GLOSSARY

PEOPLE

Barbara – Education Manager
Oversees Education department and responsible for education initiatives and community outreach for the association.

Dave – Assistant Director
Oversees the operations of the association: IT, Member Services, Accounting, Human Resources, Meetings and Events, Marketing.

Gina – Marketing Manager
Responsible for membership and marketing for the association.

Joan – Communications Manager
Oversees operations of Communications department, all graphics design and print production.

Kelly – Web Developer
Supports the Senior web developer and web designer. Assists in day-to-day operations of internal web servers, database creation and maintenance.

Lisa – Careers Coordinator
Responsible for compiling and coordinating careers information for the association.

Mara – Assistant Director
Oversees the operations of the program aspects of the association: publications, graphics design, and electronic publications.

Mike – Senior Web Developer
Oversees day-to-day operations of the internal web servers, database creation and maintenance, other programming.

Pat – Graphics Designer
Supports Communications Department. Creates artwork for print production.

Stu – Executive Director
CEO equivalent. The only elected member of the staff. Also serves as the Secretary on the Board of Trustees. Oversees all aspects of the association's operations.

Susan – Meetings & Events Manager
Oversees and manages the various conferences and events the association conducts each year.

Tanya – Meetings & Events Assistant
Supports the Meetings & Events Manager. Assists in coordinating and planning for conferences and events.

Tina – Special Projects Assistant
Supports the Executive Director. Assists in day-to-day operations of the Executive Office.

KEY TERMS

Acrobat – Adobe's program for making and reading PDF files.

CFML – ColdFusion Markup Language, a scripting language for ColdFusion.

CGI – Common Gateway Interface, a standard for interfacing programs executed on a web server with the web browser.

ColdFusion – Macromedia's software for building dynamic web applications.

Dreamweaver – Macromedia's software for web authoring.

Firefox – Mozilla's web browsing client.

Fireworks – Macromedia's image-editing and web design application.

FTP (File Transfer Protocol) – Protocol commonly used to exchange files over the Internet.

HTML (HyperText Markup Language) – Markup language designed for the creation of web pages.

HTTP (HyperText Transfer Protocol) – Method by which information is conveyed on the web.

Illustrator – Adobe's software for creating artwork for print and the web.

Imageready – Adobe's web tool application that comes as a companion to Photoshop.

International Association of Webmaster (IWA) – Professional trade association providing professional development opportunities for web professionals around the globe. Homepage: http://www.iwanet.org/

Internet Explorer – Microsoft's web browsing client.

JavaScript – Scripting language used to develop client and server Internet applications.

Majordomo – Mailing list software that manages Internet mailing lists.

Mockup – A model or prototype.

MSN Messenger – Microsoft's instant messaging client for Windows computers.

National Association of Photoshop Professionals (NAPP) – Professional trade association focused on providing training, education, and news-related to Adobe Photoshop professionals around the globe. Homepage: http://www.photoshopuser.com/

Netscape – Originally Netscape Communications Corporation's web browsing client, now developed by AOL.

Newbie – A newcomer, an inexperienced or ignorant user.

Opera – Opera Software's web browsing client.

Outlook – Microsoft's email application that comes with the Microsoft Office suite.

PDF – Adobe's Portable Document Format.

Photoshop – Adobe's professional image-editing software.

PowerPoint – Microsoft's slideshow presentation application that comes with the Microsoft Office suite.

SQL – Structured Query Language

Telecommuting – Working from a location outside of the office of employer.

URL (Uniform Resource Locator) – web address (ie. http://www.ggcinc.com/)

WebTrends – Web log analyzer used to create customized reports on a variety of statistics.